THE MARK OF JESUS

THE MARK OF JESUS

LOVING IN A WAY THE WORLD CAN SEE

TIMOTHY GEORGE
JOHN WOODBRIDGE

MOODY PUBLISHERS
CHICAGO

All Scripture quotations, unless otherwise indicated, are taken from the *Holy Bible, New International Version*®. NIV®. Copyright © 1973, 1978, 1984 by International Bible Society. Used by permission of Zondervan Publishing House. All rights reserved.

Scripture quotations marked THE MESSAGE are from *The Message*, copyright © by Eugene H. Peterson 1993, 1994, 1995. Used by permission of NavPress Publishing Group.

Scripture quotations marked ESV are taken from *The Holy Bible, English Standard Version*. Copyright © 2000, 2001 by Crossway Bibles, a division of Good News Publishers. Used by permission. All rights reserved.

Scripture quotations marked KJV are taken from the King James Version.

Library of Congress Cataloging-in-Publication Data

George, Timothy.
    The mark of Jesus : loving in a way the world can see / Timothy George, John Woodbridge.
        p. cm.
    Includes bibliographical references.
    ISBN-13: 978-0-8024-8123-8
    1. Agapé. 2. Love—Religious aspects—Christianity. 3. Jesus Christ—Example. I. Woodbridge, John D., 1941- II. Title.

BV4639.G45 2005
241'.4—dc22

                                                                2004030763

ISBN: 0-8024-8123-X
EAN/ISBN-13: 978-0-8024-8123-8

3 5 7 9 10 8 6 4 2

Printed in the United States of America

In piam memoriam

Francis A. Schaeffer (1912–1984)

Kenneth S. Kantzer (1917–2002)

Contents

Imagine: A World Without God

In 1971, the song "Imagine" quickly climbed the musical charts. Composed by the late John Lennon of Beatles' fame, "Imagine" is hauntingly wistful. Its lyrics project a vision of an ideal world in which "all the people" are "living life in peace."

Listeners are beckoned to "imagine" what this peaceful world would be like. According to Lennon, there would be "no need for greed or hunger." Furthermore, this peaceful world would have an atheistic orientation. Belief in heaven and hell would disappear. In fact, there would be no "religion" at all.

A number of assumptions apparently shaped Lennon's vision: (1) Religion can be dispensed with. There is no God; (2) heaven and hell can be dispensed with. What we experience in this life is all there is; (3) religion destroys peace. Its history is beset by bloody wars, repeated rounds of persecution, and waves of bigotry; and (4) people without religion would be good and generous. They would share their material possessions with each other, thereby ending greed or hunger.

In the early 1970s, the song's vision of a world at peace struck a responsive chord with numerous young people of the Vietnam War generation. The vision appeared to mirror well their idealistic aspirations for a world in which social, racial, and economic equality and justice might finally reign—a secular millennium, if you will. "Imagine" quickly became one of the most listened-to songs of all time and assumed its place as a cherished, atheistic anthem of the "post-Christian" West.

WHEN CHRISTIAN INFLUENCE
LEFT FRENCH EDUCATION

A few years after "Imagine" was released, one of the present authors attended a conference in France at which eminent university academics engaged in lively, informal conversations. During a free flowing discussion, a distinguished scholar observed that he and the twenty-five academics seated around the table were the last professors teaching at major universities in France to have received instruction in Christian catechisms as children. Now their students at universities often came from secular homes. Others were Muslims, Hindus, or Buddhists, who did not know even the basic rudiments of the Christian faith. A professor of medieval history volunteered that he had been obliged to create a simple dictionary of Christian terms for his students, some of whom were unfamiliar with words like *Trinity, atonement,* and *Eucharist.* In earlier decades he had assumed that students in French universities understood basic Christian vocabulary.

As the professors gazed at one another across the table, you sensed you were witnessing a group of individuals coming to a collective realization that they were a dying breed: No new generation of catechized professors would replace them. Much like the last generation of dinosaurs, they were doomed to extinction. They viewed themselves as representing the very last outcropping of Christendom's long-standing influence on French education.

They could understand why the lyrics of "Imagine" with its atheistic thrust made sense to many of their students: The students had received little instruction in the Christian faith. Moreover, Marxist students in particular viewed the Christian religion as an ideological tool which for centuries the rich and powerful had used to keep the working poor in an impoverished state. Many of them participated in the student revolts of May/June 1968 in which, like revolutionaries of old, they had torn up streets, built barricades, and fought police (*"les flics"*) in an effort to control the Latin Quarter of Paris.

Historian Philip Jenkins of Penn State University has studied the secularizing trends in the "liberal West." Even while making the startling claim that within a quarter century the number of Christians worldwide will grow to 2.6 billion, "making Christianity by far the world's largest faith," he observes that Christianity has lost considerable ground in the West: "Christians are facing a shrinking population in the liberal West and a growing majority of the traditional Rest. During the past half-century the critical centers of the Christian world have moved decisively to Africa, to Latin America, and to Asia. The balance will never shift back."[1]

PEACE WITHOUT GOD

Indeed, at the beginning of the new millennium, many westerners continue to endorse a key premise of Lennon's "Imagine": No religion is a precondition for world peace. Well-respected commentators argue that world religions have fomented warfare, fostered injustice, and fractured relationships between persons. In *Revelation, the Religions, and Violence* (2000), Leo D. Lefebure writes: "Many of the violent conflicts in the world today involve religious animosities. Indeed, the history of the encounters among the world's religions is filled with distrust and hatred and vengeance."[2] Others strenuously defend the thesis that "religion" (including the Christian faith) has no place in the public arena. Religion should be placed in the private sphere, if ever an era of peace, justice, and unity is to occur. After all, in the 1960s was it not religion in the main that had provoked warfare between Protestants and Roman Catholics in Northern Ireland? Did not John Lennon's 1971 "Imagine" provide a simple but profound solution to the problem of worldwide religious warfare? Indeed, post-Christians say it's time to abolish religion altogether from the public sphere.

Obviously, from a Christian point of view, the simple but provocative lyrics of "Imagine," advocating a world without religion, furnish exactly the wrong prescription for the spiritual sickness of sin with which we are all mortally afflicted. The lyrics tragically divert people away from the true source of peace: Jesus Christ, whom the Scriptures call the Prince of Peace. They direct people away the gospel of Jesus Christ, a "gospel of peace" (Ephesians 6:15).

How do we gain a hearing for the gospel of Jesus Christ from millions of people in a post-Christian Europe or in the United States, Canada, Australia, or elsewhere who may think that religion is an obstacle to peace, or who may be captivated by materialism's siren calls, or who may think that all religions equally lead to God?

For that matter, how do we present the Gospel to the devoted followers of other world religions, like Muslims who believe that Christendom launched horrendous Crusades in the past? How do we interact with the criticism that the West is invading other regions perversely by exporting decadence through its movies, television programming, music, and advertisements?

One thing we cannot do. We cannot write off certain "nonbelievers" and followers of other world religions who criticize Christianity by saying that the "hardness of hearts" is so deep we should not attempt to reach them with Christ's Gospel. No warrant in Scripture exists for this line of thought.

No one is beyond the reach of the Holy Spirit's gracious intervention or wooing. Compelling evidence comes in the form of one of Christianity's harshest critics, Jean-Paul Sartre. Toward the end of his life, the existentialist philosopher confessed a belief in the Christian faith, according to fellow philosopher Henri Guitton. An interviewer for the magazine *Paris Match* posed this question to Guitton: "Do you mean to say that Sartre, this living symbol of atheistic philosophy, would be, without us knowing it, a defender of the Christian faith?"

"Yes," Guitton responded, "hardly any one knows that at the end of his life, when he was blind and practically paralyzed, he gave an interview in the course of which he clearly said that he had been wrong throughout his life and that henceforth he wished to witness in favor of the existence of God. But, if no one has ever known anything about this reversal, it is because Simone de Beauvoir did everything possible to stop the publication of this interview. But I am sure that someday the truth will be established."[3]

Simone de Beauvoir, Sartre's atheistic companion, understood only too well what a devastating blow it would be for Sartre's atheistic followers to learn that he had apparently become a Christian.

THE CHRISTIANS' RESPONSE

Given the secular culture of the "liberal West," what can we do? First, moved by a spirit of love, compassion, and obedience to Christ, *we must continue to preach the Gospel in the post-Christian West as well as any other region* of the world. Christ commissioned His disciples to take the Gospel into the entire world. He did not designate any particular region of the world or people group as "off-limits" or "unreachable," such as the populations of the "liberal West." The Gospel, "the power of God for . . . salvation" (Romans 1:16), can break the stony hardness of anyone's heart, even that of a Sartre.

We are all ambassadors for Christ. Each one of us is commissioned to bring the gospel of Jesus Christ into our own particular neighborhood at home or overseas.

Second, we need to continue to create innovative new tools to present the Gospel clearly. The *Jesus* film provides an example of just such an excellent tool. Tens of thousands of people throughout the world have come to know Christ as Lord and Savior while watching this film.

Third, we need to provide means whereby young evangelicals can become excellent communicators in the arts, sciences, and government. We need gifted and respected Christian writers, journalists, artists and musicians, teachers, businesspeople, scientists, government officials, and church workers.

Fourth, we need to draw up well-crafted apologetic works in which the truth claims of the Christian faith and ethics are set forth persuasively

and winsomely. Some non-Christians have not heard thoughtful responses to their questions about the intellectual viability of the Christian faith. In our own day, the books of Lee Strobel, Josh McDowell, and
Phillip E. Johnson, among others, have provided Christians with helpful material with which to address their own questions and those of non-
Christians.

Fifth, we need to create works particularly well suited for "postmoderns"
who do put much stock in the historical arguments for Christ's resurrection or in theistic proofs such as the design argument. Philosopher
Alvin Plantinga has given a splendid example of what a persuasive cri-
tique of "methodological atheism" might represent. Likewise, we need
a carefully constructed cultural analysis that helps us understand the
mind-set and values of those peoples in non-Western cultures who are
neither postmodern and not especially impressed by rational apologetic
presentations nor are "western" in their thinking.

In God's grace, evangelical Christians are even now engaged in many
thoughtful initiatives to reach the unchurched and the followers of other
religions with the marvelous gospel of Jesus Christ. Literally thousands
of churches and ministries (from storefront churches in New York City
to the Billy Graham Association) are faithfully proclaiming this Gospel
throughout the world. Some of these believers are doing so at great
sacrifice—even at the cost of their lives. Our hearts give thanks to the
Lord for these wonderful churches and ministries.

AND YET . . .

And yet . . . and yet. Despite our best efforts in communicating the
gospel of Jesus Christ—in undertaking economic development programs;
in building churches, schools, and hospitals; in drawing up culturally
sensitive Christian literature—we may discover to our dismay that many
non-Christians dismiss our evangelistic initiatives out of hand. What's
more troubling, they apparently feel little sense of loss in doing so.

Encountering this rejection, our immediate reaction could be quite
pained and defensive. We might attempt to explain this dismissal by saying that non-Christians reject the Gospel due to their spiritual blindness

and desire to run their own lives. And certainly this is ultimately true. We are all born rebels and have sinned.

Or we may attempt to explain a lack of receptivity to the Gospel as the result of our difficulty in placing a reasonable, carefully argued defense of Christianity before the general public.

THE CHARGES OF HYPOCRISY . . .

Another explanation, however, also goes a long way to account for the lack of receptivity by non-Christians to our presentation of the gospel of Jesus. It focuses upon how Christians have lived in the past and how they are living in the present.

Many non-Christians are convinced that Christians are inveterate hypocrites. One cartoon in *The New Yorker* (January 26, 2004) cleverly exploits this widespread sentiment. The cartoon shows a prisoner in a cell turning to another who is sitting on a cot. The first prisoner has apparently just asked the second man why he is in jail. The second responds cryptically: "I'm between congregations." With a deft touch, the cartoonist had scored Christians—in this instance, a hypocritical clergy member—for not practicing what they preach. What's worse, the cartoonist assumed that the readers of *The New Yorker*, so aware of Christians' flawed reputations, would not need a lengthy explanation to reveal the cartoon's barb.

Moreover, like John Lennon, some non-Christians do not think that Christians have promoted the cause of peace, let alone goodness and righteousness. Christians' claims about Jesus Christ as the Prince of Peace ring hollow to them.

Look at the Christians' track record, they say. World history provides irrefutable evidence that Christians have promoted religious warfare, seized lands from native peoples, profited from the institution of slavery, fomented anti-Semitism, and oppressed women.

Now, as Christians, this familiar list of criticisms hurts. We know that it packs unvarnished generalizations that claim far too much. We can cite numerous counterexamples of Christians who sought peace, who fought against slavery, who—at the risk of their lives—hid Jews from the

Nazis during World War II, who worked for women's rights. But the perception remains among many non-Christians that the track record of Christians, in fact, sustains their contention. And perceptions, even if misformed, can shape people's attitudes.

In this light, non-Christians often feel a sense of moral rectitude and intellectual superiority when they encounter Christians whom they suppose to be "hypocritical" and "gullible." Meanwhile, the non-Christians sometimes view themselves as rational, serene, generous, tolerant, and humane people. They feel they are in the right, morally and intellectually, to judge the foibles and weaknesses of Christians.

. . . Intellectual Abandonment

Writing in a leading journal of thought, *The New York Review of Books,* Charles Simic, after a visit to the rural South, reassured his readers about just how backward and hypocritical Christians there were. Not worried about indulging in wholesale caricatures, he described the attitude of evangelical Protestants toward learning in a most unflattering fashion:

> Skepticism, empirical evidence, and book learning are in low esteem among the Protestant evangelicals. To ask about the laws of cause and effect would be a sin. They reject modern science and dream of a theocratic state where such blasphemous subject matter would be left out from the school curriculum. Their ideal, as a shrewd young fellow told me in Tuscaloosa, is unquestioning obedience and complete conformity in matters of religion and politics. Their complaint about so-called secular humanism is that it permits teachers and students too much freedom of thought and opinion. If evangelicals haven't gone around smashing TV sets and computers, it is because they recognize their power to spread their message. Aside from that they would like to secede intellectually from the rest of the world.[4]

Simic was no less scathing in generalizing about the evangelical preachers he heard: "The men doing the preaching had made millions saving souls and had no qualms offering themselves as a model to emulate. Their lack of humility was astonishing. I'm flying high, the faces said, because God has time for me."[5]

Non-Christians often view themselves as stoic realists who look squarely at the world as it really is and do not flinch. They are the ones who do not need the crutch of religion to help them face whatever troubles life serves up. Some may have given themselves over to a mad quest for sensual gratification, but at least they acknowledge what they have done. They are not hypocritical about their lifestyles as they believe many Christians are who cover up the fact that they do the very same things.

. . . AND FUNDAMENTALISTS WHO ARE RADICAL

More recently, a number of scholars have created another rationale that permits them to dismiss conservative Christians in a rather cavalier fashion. These scholars have grouped together "radical believers" of various world religions under the rubric "fundamentalist." They describe "fundamentalist believers" as upholding a belief in the infallibility of their holy books. These true "believers" allegedly think they can interpret infallibly the infallible book of their particular religion and thereafter arrive at a set of ethics that is likewise infallible. This approach dooms these "true believers" on several negative counts. They supposedly become militant and fanatical as defenders of their religion in its purest, original forms. They allegedly turn aggressive and strike back against the "true believers" of other religions, against "moderates" of their own faith, and against the purveyors of secular culture.

According to this school of thought, "fundamentalists" are also "modernists" who interpret their religion using modern categories of thought and communication media. Despite their names, the "fundamentalists" depart from the fundamentals of their faiths as the earliest founders of their religions taught these fundamentals.

Tariq Ali, a brilliant political analyst, provides an example of this kind of thinking. Raised in a well-to-do Muslim home, Ali, now a self-proclaimed atheist, entitles his provocative study of "Western fundamentalism" and "Islamic fundamentalism" *The Clash of Fundamentalisms:*

Crusades, Jihads and Modernity (2002). Although Ali has his own set of intellectual objections to the truth claims of various world religions, he is particularly concerned about what the followers of various world religions do as "fundamentalist" fanatics.

Often, secular critics of world religions hesitate to criticize harshly the actual creeds of these religions. Such an approach would reveal that they are intolerant themselves. Rather, the critics frequently target the practice of certain "fundamentalist" followers of world religions. In particular, they claim that these "disciples" are fanatical and dangerous and pursue goals and tactics that are, in fact, contrary to the original teachings and precepts (the fundamentals) of the founders of these religions.

This kind of analysis satisfies and persuades many secular persons that they are in the right. They are on the side of humanity, scholarship, and justice; they are tolerant and peace loving; they do not need to examine the tired truth claims of Christianity, for example, because many of its followers are essentially hypocritical, fanatical distorters of the true teachings of Jesus.

Professors Louis Bolce and Gerald De Maio of Baruch College have coined the term *anti-fundamentalists* for these secular people in the United States. As defined in "The God Vote," an article in *The Atlantic,* "Anti-fundamentalists are typically secularists or religious liberals whose political behavior is influenced by a deep antipathy toward religious conservatives; they made up 35% of [presidential candidate Al] Gore's white voters in 2000."[6]

Moreover, many Europeans are likewise worried about "American fundamentalists." Polling suggests that a majority of the French, for example, are genuinely fearful that "Muslim fundamentalists" and "Christian fundamentalists" will precipitate a world war as they struggle for world dominance.

Secular individuals often feel fully justified and genuinely at ease in rejecting out of hand any presentation of the gospel of Jesus Christ. Once again, they *know* Christians who present this Gospel are hypocrites, not practicing what they preach.

The Telling Mark of Love

Is there any way to dislodge what we will call the "hypocrisy" stumbling block from the thinking of non-Christians today? Francis Schaeffer put his finger on what he called a "final apologetic," well equipped to remove this stumbling block. It focused on how we as Christians get along with each other and with non-Christians. He observed that this is an "apologetic" Christians have rarely used.

In *The Mark of the Christian,* Schaeffer proposed that non-Christians do have a right to expect that what we Christians say about love and peace and righteousness is what we, in fact, practice. Referring to how Christians treat each other, he wrote: "The world has a right to look upon us as we, as true Christians, come to practical differences and it should be able to observe that we do love each other. Our love must have a form that the world may observe, it must be seeable."

Why does the world have this right to expect that we love one another? Schaeffer cited Christ's specific commandment that stipulates the "mark of the Christian" we are all to bear:

> A new command I give you: Love one another. As I have loved you, so you must love one another. By this all men will know that you are my disciples, if you love one another. (John 13:34–35)

> My prayer is not for them alone. I pray also for those who will believe in me through their message, that all of them may be one, Father, just as you are in me and I am in you. . . . May they be brought to complete unity to let the world know that you sent me and have loved them as you have loved me. (John 17:20–21, 23)

Schaeffer has summarized well what this teaching of Christ means for us in practical terms:

> We as Christians are called upon to love *all* men as neighbors, loving them as ourselves. Second, that we are to love all the Christian brothers in a way that the world may observe. This means showing love to our

brothers in the midst of our differences—great or small—loving our brothers when it costs us something, loving them even under times of tremendous emotional tension, loving them in a way the world can see. In short, we are to practice and exhibit the holiness of God and the love of God, for without this we grieve the Holy Spirit. Love—and the unity it attests to—is the mark Christ gave Christians to wear before the world. Only with this mark may the world know that Christians are indeed Christians and Jesus was sent by the Father.[7]

The Mark of Jesus

In a way difficult for us to fathom, how we as Christians relate to one another has a direct bearing upon whether the world will know that Jesus comes from the Father. When this incredibly important point is grasped, we begin to understand that we ignore this neglected "apologetic" to our great loss. Neither our evangelistic efforts, nor our social action, nor our apologetic efforts will receive God's full blessing if we do not evidence the fruits of the Holy Spirit in our relations with each other as believers. The mark of Jesus in us is crucial, and it is compelling.

Many evangelical Christians do demonstrate this love for their Christian brothers and sisters in daily life. As we shall see, sociologist Christian Smith has found that evangelical Christians are the strongest group of religious people in the United States when it comes not only to upholding orthodox beliefs but to walking their talk in doing good to others. At the same time, we must humbly confess that some of us as evangelicals are not especially well known for our "observable love" in the way we treat each other. Schaeffer puts the matter this way: "I want to say with all my heart that as we struggle with the proper preaching of the gospel in the midst of the 20th century, the importance of observable love must come into our message. We must not forget the final apologetic."

Francis Schaeffer observed that there were few books or articles devoted to reflection upon this apologetic. Since the days he wrote *The Mark of the Christian,* a number of valuable studies have emerged that do help us think through what this apologetic might look like in practice.

The Mark of Jesus seeks to further unpack what this apologetic is and how it might play out in the various situations we face, both in our encounters with other believers as well as our lives with nonbelievers.

It is our contention that when Christians work together for a common Christ-honoring cause, sometimes setting aside their own wishes in favor of others' wishes and esteeming others better than themselves, great good can be accomplished. Egos are harnessed, personal ambitions throttled, wise consensus may be reached, and the body of Christ is strengthened. A watching world begins to see Christians loving each other and is impressed. The unity of the body of Christ is made more visible. Evangelism advances more rapidly in consequence.

IMAGINE . . . HARMONY AMONG CHRISTIANS

A picture of Christians working together in harmony may initially strike some of us as unrealistic as John Lennon's imagined, secular world of peace. Immediately, our minds are flooded with questions that make even contemplating such a picture problematic. Whose definition of a Christian should be used in determining if "real Christians" are the people described as loving each other and working together? Is it not a utopian vision to imagine that Christians in general could exist in unity, given the fractious relations Christians have maintained with one another for the last two millennia? Are not denominations themselves testimonies to meaningful divisions that have developed within Christendom? Have not we as evangelicals become so accustomed to divisions within Christ's church that we feel helpless to challenge the status quo; that is, the way things presently are? Are not some of our divisions inevitable and even advisable? Are not some of us determined to uphold true doctrine, whereas we believe other Christians, even though they are basically orthodox, entertain beliefs that are unbiblical or at least less than faithful?

Still other questions arise regarding Christians working and worshiping together. Is there anything wrong with our desire to worship with people more like ourselves racially and economically speaking than with others with whom we have little in common save the Christian faith itself? How would we know if we have loved one another sufficiently well to meet the standard Christ has established? Would this standard be reached only if there were one visible world church evident to the watching world? Is a quest for Christian unity simply a form of wrongheaded and warmed-over ecumenism that leads to a lowest-common-denominator Christianity, if Christianity at all? From whence comes the power to love some other Christians with whom we may have a profound personal grievance?

These are serious and legitimate questions. They cannot be easily swept under the rug. They impinge on our thinking when we begin contemplating what it means for us to so love one another in such a way that the world takes notice and recognizes we are Christ's disciples.

This book does not attempt to answer all these questions. Rather, it addresses more directly a set of pivotal issues related to these questions —issues that either hinder us from wearing the mark of the Christian or hinder non-Christians from seeing that mark upon us. We do not claim that our treatment of these issues represents the last word on them. Undoubtedly, wiser people than we can provide wiser analysis. Nonetheless, we hope this discussion will encourage each one of us to pray that the Holy Spirit will renew within us our desire to love the Lord our God with all our hearts, souls, and minds and our neighbors as ourselves.

A PREVIEW

Chapter 1, "The Christian's Mark," helps us understand better the traits we are called to evidence if we are Christ's disciples. Chapter 2, "Loving Your Neighbor When It Seems Impossible," provides illustrations of ways we can seek to love others from whom we feel alienated or with whom we have little in common. Chapter 3, "Evangelical Unity," analyzes the issue of how evangelicals can demonstrate love for one another when they disagree even among themselves on issues of importance.

Chapters 4 and 5 consider the charges of hypocrisy and radicalism in the Christian church. In chapter 6, we look at how bearing the "mark of Jesus" can open up doors of opportunity for friendships with and ministry to people of other religions. The conclusion calls upon every follower of Christ to wear the "mark of Jesus" in today's world—a world awash in anxiety. Whether non-Christians will listen to our presentation of the Gospel often depends in a significant measure upon whether they see us bearing the "mark of Jesus." They determine whether we bear that mark by the evidence of *costly love* we display to other believers and to themselves.

In the twenty-first century, if Christians are to work in harmony, believers of whatever nationality, race, or economic background will need to bear the "mark of Jesus." Christians are called to have a passionate love for God and their neighbors. Jesus teaches that we are to love the Lord our God with all our hearts, souls, and minds and our neighbor as ourselves. This is healthy, passionate religion. It can produce deep compassion, great sacrifice, and beneficent actions for fellow believers and non-Christians. By contrast, passionate religion (extremism) not prompted and constrained by the Holy Spirit can end in terrible fanatical and destructive behavior. The twenty-first century may very well see both kinds of passionate religion. Philip Jenkins observes: "The twenty-first century will almost certainly be regarded by future historians as a century in which religion replaced ideology as the prime animating and destructive force in human affairs."

The Christian's Mark

Contrary to what you might have been told, the Bible teaches that we should care about what other people think of us. We should not "repay anyone evil for evil," but "do what is right *in the eyes of everybody*" (Romans 12:17, italics added). Writing to the Philippians from prison, Paul declared that his difficult circumstances were really serving the advance of the Gospel because it had "become clear throughout the whole palace guard and to everyone else that I am in chains for Christ" (Philippians 1:13).

The early Christians were concerned, and rightly so, about the impressions unbelievers—"outsiders"—might carry away from a visit to their worship service (1 Corinthians 14:23–24). And, among the pastoral qualifications set forth in the New Testament, is this one: "He must also have a good reputation with outsiders" (1 Timothy 3:7). Jesus

Himself said that we are to let our light shine before others so that they can see our good works (Matthew 5:16).

This does not mean that we should trim our convictions or shape our behavior in order to curry favor with the world around us. But we should never forget that Jesus does give the world the right to decide whether we are true Christians based upon our observable love for one another. "By this all men will know that you are my disciples, if you love one another" (John 13:35). How else *could* they know? They cannot peer into our hearts. But they can read our lips, see our lives, and observe the way we relate to one another. Above all else, Jesus said, this is the telling mark of a Christian.

In the next two chapters, we are going to look at some of the common charges and misperceptions often leveled against Christians by a watching world. In this chapter, however, we want to begin by looking at ourselves.

Why are Christians so often at each other's throats? Why are so many church splits centered around personalities and petty politics? Why is Christian unity so seldom preached about in Bible-believing churches? We shall answer these questions by looking at Paul's interaction with the dynamic but fractious congregation at Corinth.

In the course of his second missionary journey, the apostle Paul had a sudden change of itinerary. Instead of continuing east, as he had originally planned, he responded to his vision of a Macedonian man begging him, "Come over and help us" (see Acts 16:9). Crossing the Aegean Sea, he began to preach the Gospel on European soil. First to Philippi, then to Thessalonica, Berea, Athens, and finally to Corinth, Paul brought the message of Jesus Christ.

THE MESS AT CORINTH

Corinth was a bustling seaport at the crossroads of the shipping lanes between East and West. Here Roman power met Greek culture mingled with Oriental mysticism and gnostic spirituality. In Corinth, the drinking was hard, the economy was corrupt, the sex was sizzling, and the politics was cutthroat. Everything was up for grabs. Corinth was a postmodern city before postmodern was cool.

Here in this caldron of sensuality and syncretism, a church was born; "the church of God in Corinth," Paul called it. Paul was not only the evangelist who planted this church; he was also its founding pastor. For eighteen months, he stayed with its members, sharing their joys and sorrows, their heartaches and struggles as only a pastor can share such things. How else are we to understand a verse like this: "I wrote you out of great distress and anguish of heart and with many tears, not to grieve you but to let you know the depth of my love for you" (2 Corinthians 2:4)? Again, he wrote, "I speak as to my children. . . . Make room for us in your hearts" (2 Corinthians 6:13; 7:2).

Paul's heart was broken because he had received a report that the church in Corinth, the church he had planted and nurtured and fathered in God, was hopelessly *divided*. Paul's first letter to the Corinthians bristles with conflict. Many of the issues that troubled that New Testament congregation are with us still. Beginning at the end of First Corinthians and working our way back to the opening chapters, we can identify at least fourteen major sources of quarreling, bickering, and dissension in this church:

Chapter 16   Chapter 16 opens with a word about *money*. Paul is taking a collection to send to the beleaguered Christians in Jerusalem, and he wants the brothers and sisters at Corinth to contribute to this missionary offering. Some people in this church had pledged to support the mission offering but had now gone back on their promise. Others were contributing begrudgingly, out of a sense of mere duty, rather than from generosity and joy. So Paul writes back to remind them that "God loves a cheerful giver" and that God Himself is the greatest giver of all, for He has blessed us with the "inexpressible gift" of His own Son (2 Corinthians 9:7, 15 ESV).

Chapter 15   First Corinthians 15 is about *eschatology*, the second coming of Christ. Many Christians in our day are divided over these same issues. Should we interpret the millennium as a literal one-thousand-year reign of Christ on earth or as a figurative term referring to the age of the church or to God's sovereign rule over history? When will the Antichrist be revealed? How does the state of Israel relate to God's prophetic timetable? In Corinth, the arguments were about whether there would be a resurrection in the future, the nature of our glorified bodies, and baptism for the dead.

Chapter 14	Chapter 14 is about *worship wars.* What about speaking in tongues? Raucous business meetings? Women preachers? "When you come together," Paul declares, "each one of you has a hymn, a lesson, a revelation, a tongue, or an interpretation" (verse 26 ESV). Confusion and chaos was the order of the day.
Chapter 12	Chapter 12 is about *spiritual gifts:* healing, miracles, and prophecy.
Chapter 11	Chapter 11 is about *clothing,* specifically, feminine fashions: What should women wear to church?
Chapters 10–11	Chapter 10—and 11 too (verses 17–33)—deal with *the Lord's Supper.* This was not just a liturgical dispute over the proper eucharistic ritual. It concerned the very nature of the fellowship the believers at Corinth shared with one another around the Lord's Table. Some of the richer members were gorging themselves at a sumptuous dinner, while the poor members, including slaves, went home hungry. This disparity made a mockery of their participation in the body and blood of Christ symbolized in the bread and wine of the Lord's Supper.
Chapters 8–9	Chapters 8 and 9 deal with a controverted issue of food offered to idols. At the heart of this dispute was a deeper issue: *How sensitive should Christians be to one another? How careful should they be not to give offense?*
Chapter 7	Chapter 7 takes up *family issues: divorce, marriage, sexuality, and celibacy.*

Chapter 6	Chapter 6 deals with *how Christians are to settle disputes with one another* in a litigious society. Should Christians sue one another in the secular law courts?
Chapter 5	Chapter 5 is about *sexual immorality and the need for church discipline* within the congregation.
Chapter 4	Chapter 4 refers to *pride and arrogance among leaders in the church.*
Chapter 3	Chapter 3 is about *spiritual immaturity.*
Chapter 2	Chapter 2 warns against *the danger of intellectualizing the Gospel.*
Chapter 1	Chapter 1 is about *party strife and cliques within the congregation.*

Paul wanted the church in Corinth to "be united in the same mind and the same judgment" (1 Corinthians 1:10 ESV). But, in fact, a four-way split had developed within the church. "One of you says, 'I follow Paul'; another, 'I follow Apollos'; another, 'I follow Cephas'; still another, 'I follow Christ'" (1 Corinthians 1:12). The Paul party, the Peter party, and the Apollos party had all made celebrities out of their favorite preachers. The church at Corinth was in danger of being seduced by the pagan culture around it, and ministers of the Gospel turned into glamorous heroes—"jocks in the pulpit." God had given these leaders to the church to be "servants" (3:5), but instead they had become a source of enmity and division.

The results are no different with a fourth group, the Christ party, who claimed that they were the ones who really belonged to Christ, unlike the others. But their confidence wasn't really in Christ; it was in themselves—their orthodoxy, their uprightness, their special status. With reference to this group, Paul later wrote: "If anyone is confident that he belongs to Christ, he should consider again that we belong to Christ just as much as he" (2 Corinthians 10:7). In other words, Paul said to them: "The fact that you 'belong to Christ' is wonderful. This makes grace more immeasurable; it does not make you more memorable!"

THE OVERARCHING SIN: PRIDE

At the heart of all these divisions was the sin of pride. In the name of purity, tradition, correctness, and spirituality, the church at Corinth became puffed up. In their pride, they sniped at each other and walked around on stilts above their Christian brothers. During the Reformation, Martin Luther reminded those who wanted to exalt him above measure: "The first thing I ask is that people should not make use of my name and should not call themselves Lutherans but Christians. How did I, poor stinking bag of maggots that I am, come to the point where people call the children of Christ by my evil name?"

When the world looks at us, as it did at the Christians in Corinth, what does it see? Do we come across as genuine servants of Christ, those willing to put the interests of others ahead of our own? Or are we better known for our partisan competitions, personal rivalries, and cliquish exclusivism? What does Jesus think when He looks down on all of this?

What does Paul say to the warring factions in Corinth? We might expect him to say something like this: "You folks need to back the party that bears my name. I am the founding pastor of your church! These other people, followers of Peter, Apollos, and the so-called Christ party, they're all newcomers, interlopers. When the next church business meeting comes around, we need to get out all of the Pauline folk to vote the right way!" But, instead, Paul says to all of these groups: "Come down from your wisdom, your arrogance, pride, and condescension toward your brothers and sisters. Come down to the cross, where all of our human pretensions are shown to be folly, where God alone is great, and Jesus alone is Lord."

THREE QUESTIONS

In this context, Paul asks three crucial questions in 1 Corinthians 1:13.

1. *"Is Christ divided?"* Eugene Peterson translates this text: "Has the Messiah been chopped up in little pieces so we can each have a relic all our own?" (THE MESSAGE). You're acting, Paul says, as though Christ was

a chunk of meat, a commodity you can buy down at the butcher shop, something to be hacked and diced up and passed around like hors d'oeuvres at a party! The Greek word here is *memeristai,* which means to divide into parties or sects. We could translate Paul's question this way: Is Christ a partisan? Is Christ sectarian? The very idea, of course, is ludicrous. Christ is not divisible.

The church of the New Testament is the church of the undivided Christ. This fact alone separated Christianity from the pagan religions of the ancient Mediterranean world. Wherever one looked in Corinth, there loomed polytheism. On top of the nearby mountain stood the great temple of Aphrodite, the goddess of love. The cult of the Roman emperor also flourished there, as did many of the mystery religions imported from Egypt and the East. No wonder Paul could say that in the world there are many "gods" and many "lords." Yet for us, he insisted, "there is one God, the Father, from whom are all things and for whom we exist and one Lord, Jesus Christ, through whom are all things and through whom we exist" (8:6 ESV). Jesus Christ cannot be divided, because there is only one God, and Jesus is divine not in the sense of the Greek gods, whose divinity was mutable and contingent, but rather as the One who has come from "the bosom of the Father" to disclose the one eternal God who has forever known Himself as the Father, the Son, and the Holy Spirit.

Here is Paul's point: There is a direct correlation between ecclesiology and Christology, between the church and its heavenly head, Jesus Christ. And when we live in rancor, bitterness, and enmity with one another, we are sinning not only against our brother and sister, but also against Christ. This is a lesson Paul learned on the first day he became a Christian. On his way to persecute believers in Damascus, he was suddenly halted by the risen Christ, who asked him, "Saul, Saul, why are you persecuting me?" (Acts 9:4 ESV). He might well have responded, "I am not persecuting You. I'm on my way to arrest these miserable Christians!" But Jesus' question to Saul implies that it is not possible to hurt those who belong to Him, those who have been redeemed by His blood, without also hurting Him. "Whatever you did for one of the least of these brothers of mine, you did it for me" (Matthew 25:40). This perspective elevates the question of disunity and conflict among believers to an en-

tirely new level. Would we say about Jesus what we have said about some
of our colleagues, friends, and fellow church members? Would we direct our anger at Him the way we have held grudges or harbored bitter
thoughts against them? How would we act at the next elders' meeting if
Jesus showed up?

2. *"Was Paul crucified for you?"* Here Paul reminds the Corinthian believers that their lives in Christ are inextricably bound up with what happened one Friday afternoon in Jerusalem outside the gates of the city
when Jesus was impaled on a Roman cross. Why does he mention the
cross at this point? Because the cross is where all the bragging stops.
Behind all the side-choosing and sloganeering—"I am of Paul," "I am
of Apollos," etc.—was the self-assertion and self-glorification of those
who had an overweening confidence in their own virtues and abilities:
the wise, the weighty, and the well-born, as Paul refers to them (1:26).
The common anthropological assumptions of Greek philosophy and Hel-
lenistic culture, not unlike those of the modern cult of self-esteem, greatly
valued human assertiveness in any form as a badge of excellence, strength,
and virtue. Indeed, the word *virtue* comes from the Latin *virtus,* meaning "manliness" or "worth." Physical prowess (cf. Augustine's recollec-
tion of how his pagan father Patricius used to take pride in showing off
his well-formed adolescent son in the public baths), military feats, ora-
torical abilities, intellectual acumen, political power, monetary success,
social status—all these were things to be proud of and to glory in.

But in contrast to all this, Paul held up something utterly despicable,
contemptible, and valueless by any worldly standard—the cross of Christ.
For two thousand years the cross has been so variously and beautifully
represented in Christian iconography and symbolism that it is almost impossible for us to appreciate the sense of horror and shock that must have
greeted the apostolic proclamation of a crucified Redeemer. Actually, the
Latin word *crux* was regarded as an expression so crude that no polite
Roman would utter it in public. In order to get around this difficulty,
the Romans devised a euphemistic circumlocution, "Hang him on the
unlucky tree" (*arbori infelici suspendito*), an expression that comes from
Cicero. But what the world regarded as too shameful to whisper in polite company, a detestable object used for the brutal execution of the

dregs of society, Paul declared to be the proper basis for exaltation. In the cross, and the cross alone, Paul said, he would make his boast in life and death, for all time and eternity.

Unlike some of the later Gnostic teachers, and unlike all the followers of Islam to this day, the Corinthian believers did not actually deny that Jesus was put to death on the cross. But if they did not deny the cross, they certainly de-emphasized it. They had not yet realized the ethical implications of Jesus' death for every believer: To be "in Christ," to be "crucified with Christ," implies a radical transformation within the believer, a transformation based on our identification with Jesus' once-for-all victory on the cross, but also leading to an ongoing process of mortification and self-denial. This is what Paul meant in Galatians 6:14 when he declared that not only is the world to be crucified unto us, but we also are to be crucified to the world. To be crucified to the world, in this sense, means to walk in the power of the cross, to bear the fruit of the Spirit, to live in the freedom with which Christ has set us free. To realize that Jesus, not Paul or anyone else, was crucified for us means a willingness to bear the "brand marks" of Jesus—to live under the cross. This is the only thing that we have any biblical warrant to boast about.

3. *"Were you baptized into the name of Paul?"* It may seem strange that Paul would bring baptism into the argument at this point. For centuries Christians have been deeply divided about the meaning, significance, and role of baptism in the life of the church. Should we baptize infants or only adult believers? How much water should we use—do we drip, douse, or dunk? How does baptism relate to church membership? Who is authorized to baptize, ordained ministers only or laypersons as well? Entire denominations have divided over such issues in the past, and such differences are far from resolved today, even among evangelical Christians who appeal to the authority of Scripture. No wonder that years ago Donald Bridge entitled his book about baptism *The Water That Divides*.

But something else is at stake in this passage. The question here is: *In whose name have you been baptized?* In the early church, baptism signified the transfer of loyalty from one realm into another. Baptism was far more than an initiatory rite of passage; rather, it involved a decisive transition from an old way of human life to a new and different way.

Baptism was an act of radical obedience in which a specific renunciation was made and a specific promise was given. The renunciation part, the act of publicly saying "No!" became prominent in the baptismal liturgy of the early church, as we read in documents from the late second century such as Tertullian's *On Baptism* and Hippolytus's *Apostolic Tradition.*

From these sources we learn that baptism was often done on Easter eve, following a period of intensive preparation that included fasting, prayer, and the reading of Scripture. When at last the time for baptism itself arrived, the candidate would be called upon to renounce the Devil and all his pomp. Facing westward, the direction in which the sun went down, he would exclaim, "I renounce thee, O Satan, and all thy works!" Then he would deliberately spit three times in the direction of darkness, signifying a complete break with the powers of evil and all their former claim on his life. Next, turning toward the sunrise, he would say, "And I embrace Thee, O Lord Jesus Christ!" This would be followed by immersion three times in the name of the triune God, the receiving of a new robe, anointing with oil, laying on of hands, and participation in the Lord's Supper.

Baptism was not a private ritual to be performed in secret. It was a public confession of allegiance to Jesus Christ. Baptized Christians were often singled out for persecution and were sometimes taken directly from the sacred waters of baptism to the expected bloodbath in the arena. To be baptized in the name of Jesus was risky business. It was a public declaration that "the old has gone, the new has come!" (2 Corinthians 5:17). During the Reformation, Huldrych Zwingli compared baptism to the white cross that was sewn onto the uniform of the Swiss mercenary soldiers, among whom he once served as a chaplain. Wherever the soldiers moved across the battlefield, they would be identified to all who saw them by the white cross sewn onto their red uniform. This design can still be seen today on the Swiss national flag. Baptism too, Zwingli thought, was a public badge that identified one with a particular cause. Baptism marked the believer as a member of the *militia Christi,* a soldier of the Gospel, fighting under the direction of Christ the Captain.

This was true not only of individual Christians but also of the church as the called-out people of God. Paul declared that something radically new and different had occurred within this baptized community so that "there is neither Jew nor Greek, slave nor free, male nor female" (Galatians 3:28). The three pairs of opposites Paul listed in this verse stand for the fundamental cleavages of human existence: ethnicity, economic capacity, and sexuality. Race, money, and sex are primal powers in human life. No one of them is inherently evil, yet each of these spheres of human creativity has become degraded and soiled through the perversity of sin. Nationality and ethnicity have been corrupted by pride, material blessings by greed, and sexuality by lust. This has led to the chaotic pattern of exploitation and self-destruction that marks the human story from the Tower of Babel to the streets of Baghdad and Beirut.

But the good news of the Gospel is that those who have become children of God through faith in Jesus Christ have broken free from enslavement to these controlling forces. A new standard and pattern of life now distinguishes the baptized community from the environing society all around it. Here, as nowhere else, we are empowered by the Holy Spirit to "bear one another's burdens, and so fulfill the law of Christ" (Galatians 6:2 ESV). As Gerhard Ebeling has said, the boundaries of baptism define "the existence of a place in the world where things are different: Jews and Gentiles share the same table; slaves and free citizens are treated equally as brothers and sisters; women are accorded a respect that is more substantial than a merely outward and sometimes two-edged 'equality.'"

To be baptized in the name of the crucified and risen Christ means that we have acquired a new set of comrades. We now wear the same cross on our uniforms, and we march together under the same banner, the bloodstained banner of the Lamb. We are soldiers engaged in battle, but we must not direct our weapons against one another, but against the real Enemy who has come "to steal and kill and destroy" (John 10:10).

BYPATHS TO AVOID

Paul's three questions at the beginning of his first letter to the Corinthians point to the fact that the unity of the church is grounded in the redemptive work of Jesus Christ, the one and only Lord of the church: "Is Christ divided? Was Paul crucified for you? Were you baptized in the name of Paul?" (verse 13). The answer to all these questions is a resounding no! Jesus Christ is indivisible. His atoning sacrifice alone procures our justification and right standing before God. We are baptized in the name of the Father, the Son, and the Holy Spirit, the one God we know and worship through His self-revelation in Jesus Christ.

Paul's emphasis on the oneness of the church is complemented by John's description that the spiritual oneness of believers on earth is grounded in the eternal unity of the Father and the Son (John 17:11, 21). "May they be one, Holy Father," Jesus prayed, "just as We are one" (author's paraphrase). The Trinitarian basis of Christian unity is reflected in all the orthodox creeds and confessions of the apostolic faith as well as historic patterns of prayer and worship in the early church.

All of this is great theology, but the fact remains that disgruntled believers in Corinth, and many Christians today, live as though it had no bearing on their actual conduct and relationships to one another. How can we bear the mark of a Christian when all too often those watching us observe not love and mutual concern but raucous discord and disunity? What is the way to true Christian unity?

Before giving a positive answer to this question, we want to mention three bypaths which, though tempting to many in our day, will not lead to the kind of unity we need, the kind of unity for which Jesus prayed and for which Paul yearned. The way to true Christian unity cannot be purchased at the expense of (1) moral purity, (2) theological integrity, (3) or genuine diversity.

The way to true Christian unity cannot be purchased *at the expense of moral purity.* Throughout history, the Christian church has ever lived in tension between the poles of identity and adaptability. When we focus too strongly on identity and forget adaptability, we become a "holy huddle" unmindful of the world and our mission to carry the good news of Christ to the "uttermost" limit of every culture and every people group on earth. On the other hand, when the church gravitates one-sidedly toward the pole of adaptability, it can easily lose its identity in the trends and fashions of its surrounding environment. This was precisely the problem at Corinth, and Paul, quoting from Isaiah 52, called on those believers to separate themselves from the immoral practices they had indulged in before they met Christ (2 Corinthians 6:17).

The Corinthian temptation still faces the church today. In recent years, many denominations have been torn apart by the debate over homosexuality. In the name of love and unity, some church leaders have put aside the clear teaching of Scripture on this issue, and some churches have moved to bless same-sex unions and ordain openly gay clergy. While we should all remember that homosexuals are among those persons for whom Jesus died, and that there is no place for bigotry against any person made in the image of God, we are not at liberty to set aside biblical standards for holy living and sexual purity. Stanley Grenz has written a helpful book on this subject with a title that expresses just the right response to persons engaged in or tempted toward a gay lifestyle: *Welcoming but Not Affirming* (Westminster John Knox).

The way to true Christian unity cannot be purchased *at the expense of theological integrity.* Some advocates of the mainline ecumenical movement have little patience for theological discussion and frank dialogue over doctrinal differences among the various Christian groups. They reason like this: "In a world beset by pressing social needs, racial conflict, famine, war, and a global ecological crisis, we cannot afford to dredge up the old debates that have divided Christians in the past. Let's forget about our theological differences, or at least put them on hold, so we can work together toward common goals."

While this appeal is attractive at a superficial level, it misses entirely an essential commitment of the Christian message: Truth matters. In John 17 Jesus prayed to the heavenly Father that His disciples would be one, and also that they would be sanctified through the truth (John 17:17, 22). The first premise of any honest dialogue among Christians of different denominations or theological commitments must be that any unity not based on truth is a unity not worth having. Admittedly, this conviction flies in the face of postmodernist notions of truth and the reigning ideology of theological pluralism that dominates the declining world of mainline Protestant enterprises. But it cannot be dodged if we are to be faithful to the apostolic mandate to speak the truth in love (Ephesians 4:15). On this point evangelicals can offer a hearty amen!

to the words of Cardinal Joseph Ratzinger: "Our quarreling ancestors were in reality much closer to each other when in all their disputes they still knew that they could only be servants of one truth which must be acknowledged as being as great and as pure as it has been intended for us by God."

Finally, true Christian unity cannot be purchased *at the expense of genuine diversity.* Paul makes this abundantly clear in 1 Corinthians 12, where he describes the unity of the church in terms of the interdependence and mutuality of the various members of the body. God has so created the body and tempered together its members that there should be no internal disconnect or division within the organism, but that its parts should have equal concern for each other (12:24–25). There is one body and one Spirit, just as there is one God and one Redeemer. But there are "many" gifts, many places to serve, many "diversities of operations," as the King James Version puts it (12:6).

Unity is not uniformity. To try to impose an artificial oneness on the genuine diversity we find in the body of Christ is to be blind to the many-faceted, many-colored wisdom of God.

THE WAY TO TRUE UNITY

In 1 Corinthians Paul presents the way to true Christian unity in terms of three of the greatest words of the Christian faith: Gospel, love, and grace.

First, the way of the Gospel. Near the end of this letter, Paul summarized what he has been saying to the distraught believers in Corinth:

Now, brothers, I want to remind you of the gospel I preached to you, which you received and on which you have taken your stand. By this gospel you are saved, if you hold firmly to the word I preach to you. Otherwise, you have believed in vain. For what I received I passed on to you as the first importance: that Christ died for our sins according to the Scriptures, that he was buried, that he was raised on the third day according to the Scriptures. (1 Corinthians 15:1–4)

Many implications of the Gospel are not spelled out in these short verses, but they do contain the heart of the Gospel, without which there can be no true or lasting unity. The Gospel is so simple that small children can understand it, and yet it is so profound that the wisest theologians will never be able to explain it in all of its mystery and depth.

Several years ago, a group of Bible scholars drafted a statement, "The Gospel of Jesus Christ: An Evangelical Celebration," which was endorsed by several hundred Christian leaders. That document sets forth the perspective we want to advance in this book as well:

> The Bible declares that all who truly trust in Christ and his Gospel are sons and daughters of God through grace, and hence are our brothers and sisters in Christ. . . . Christians are commanded to love each other despite differences of race, gender, privilege, and social, political, and economic background (John 13:34–35; Gal. 3:28–29), and to be of one mind wherever possible (John 17:20–21; Phil. 2:2; Rom. 14:1–15:13). We know that divisions among Christians hinder our witness in the world, and we desire greater mutual understanding and truth-speaking in love. . . . As evangelicals united in the Gospel, we promise to watch over and care for one another, to pray for and forgive one another, and to reach out in love and truth to God's people everywhere, for we are one family, one in the Holy Spirit, and one in Christ.[1]

Second, the way of love. It is not accidental that 1 Corinthians 13, the great love chapter of the Bible, comes right in between two of the most rambunctious chapters in this letter. In chapter 12, Paul had reminded the Corinthians that the body was meant to work together in harmony. It is not as a discombobulated monstrosity with legs sprouting from ears, eyes peering up from toes, and elbows growing out of the neck. Chapter 14 has shown what happens when showmanship and pride replace humility and love in the worship of God—decency and order go out the window. Right in between these two jarring lessons Paul placed his beautiful hymn about love.

In his famous exposition of this chapter, Henry Drummond referred to love as "the greatest thing in the world." First Corinthians 13 was read by Prime Minister Tony Blair at the funeral of Princess Diana at Westminster Abbey, and it is a favorite text for graduation ceremonies and weddings as well. But love, as Paul has described it, is neither romantic sentimentalism nor one of the Greek virtues doused with a thin Christian veneer. Love is the fruit of the Holy Spirit, and it manifests itself in practical ways, often with uncomfortable consequences.

For example, what does Paul mean when he says that love "is not rude . . . self-seeking, . . . easily angered, [nor] keeps [a] record of wrongs" (13:5)? We are inclined to make light of a bad temper, to dismiss it as a quirk of the personality, a family trait perhaps, nothing to be taken too seriously. But how much damage has been done within families and congregations by bitter words spoken in anger, when tempers flare and words unbecoming of Christ stream forth from inside us?

We must admit at this point that some of our great heroes of the faith have not been perfect models. For example, should Calvin have referred to the Anabaptists as "fanatics," "deluded," "scatterbrains," "asses," "scoundrels," and "mad dogs"? Was it right for Luther to refer to Pope Paul III as "His Hellishness," and to call other religious opponents spit, snot, puss, feces, urine, stench, scab, smallpox, ulcers, and syphilis?

While Jesus did refer to the scribes and Pharisees as "hypocrites" and "blind guides," who among us can presume to wear His sandals and peer into the hearts of others to make such judgments? The model of Christ we are explicitly told to take as our example is that of Jesus, the suffering servant, who "when they hurled their insults at him, he did not retaliate; when he suffered, he made no threats. Instead, he entrusted himself to him who judges justly" (1 Peter 2:23). Only twice in Paul's letters did he speak explicitly of the believer's love for God (Romans 8:28; 2 Thessalonians 3:5 ESV), although much that he said presupposes Jesus' statement about the first and greatest of the commandments. But Paul's emphasis was on the Christian's love for his fellow human beings. At one point, he goes so far as to say, "The entire law is summed up in a single command: 'Love your neighbor as yourself'" (Galatians 5:14).

Why did Paul call the selfless love of neighbor the fulfilling of the whole law? Not because it is superior to the worship and adoration of God, but rather because it is the proof of it. As Calvin correctly noted,

"God is invisible; but he represents himself to us in the brethren and in their persons demands what is due to himself. Love to men springs only from the fear and love of God."

During the debates of the Reformation, the relationship of faith, love, and good works became a matter of dispute. Did not the doctrine of justification by faith alone eliminate any place for good works in the life of the believer? Luther, Calvin, and those who followed them insisted that the fruit of justification is *faith active in love.* A living faith expresses itself in works of love, in service to the neighbor. Believers who have been made right with God by faith no longer labor under the compulsion of the law or the self-centered need to serve others as a means of enhancing their own status before God. The medieval schema of salvation declared that it was necessary for faith to be "formed by love" (*fides caritate formata*) to be effective for salvation. But Luther insisted that we are justified by faith *alone,* not by faith mingled and fortified by the loving deeds we have done for others. Thus while our love for others does not make us righteous, when one has been declared righteous by faith alone, godly love is the result.

Such love is directed in the first instance not toward God in hope of attaining some merit toward salvation, but toward one's neighbor, for "the Christian lives not in himself, but in Christ and his neighbor." Luther urged Christians to perform good works out of spontaneous love in obedience to God for the sake of others. To put it in other words, justification by faith alone frees me to love my neighbor disinterestedly, for his or her own sake, as my sister or brother, not as the calculated means to my own desired ends.

Since we no longer have to carry around the intolerable burden of self-justification, we are free "to be Christs unto one another," as Luther put it, to expend ourselves on behalf of one another, even as Christ also loved us and gave Himself for us.

Significantly, Paul does not say that God's law is summed up in the command to love our fellow Christians, but rather our neighbors. Who is our neighbor? In the light of Jesus' self-giving on the cross, we who belong to Him and bear His mark before a watching world no longer have the luxury to define our neighbors exclusively as our fellow Christians, fellow evangelicals, fellow Americans, the families in our subdivision, the members of our race, or those who agree with us politically. Our neighbors also include the loveless, the least, the unlikely.

By following Jesus, we learn to see the world through the eyes of the Savior's love. This enables us to see and relate to others not in terms of their own personal idiosyncrasies, or their sin and greediness, but in the way of Christ, who expended Himself even for those who rejected Him. The great Welsh preacher D. M. Lloyd-Jones has given an unsurpassed exposition of what it means to fulfill the law of love in service to our neighbors:

> We see them now, no longer as hateful people who are trying to rob us of our rights, or trying to beat us in the race for money, or position or fame; we see them, as we see ourselves, as the victims of sin and of Satan, as the dupes of "the God of this world," as fellow-creatures who are under the wrath of God and hell-bound. We have an entirely new view of them. We see them to be exactly as we are ourselves, and we are both in a terrible predicament. And we can do nothing; but both of us together must run to Christ and avail ourselves of his wonderful grace. We begin to enjoy it together and we want to share it together. That is how it works. It is the only way whereby we can ever do unto others as we would that they should do unto us. It is when we are really loving our neighbors as ourselves because we have been delivered from the thralldom of self, that we begin to enjoy "the glorious liberty of the children of God."[2]

Third, the way of grace. Genuine Christian unity is not something we can impose or contrive on our own. It is something given, received, and recognized by grace alone. The word *grace* is found some 150 times in the New Testament alone, and the theme of God's free, unmerited favor is woven into the fabric of Holy Scripture from Genesis to Revelation: "The grace of our Lord Jesus Christ be with you all" (Revelation 22:21 KJV). And yet the doctrine of grace itself has provoked some of the fiercest debates in the history of the church.

One of the most important of these debates took place more than three hundred years after the death of the apostle Paul. This involved a terrific struggle between Augustine, one of the greatest theologians who ever lived, and Pelagius, a British monk and moral reformer who stressed the ability of human beings to make themselves pleasing to God by obeying the law. Later, Christians referred to Augustine as *doctor gratiae,* "the teacher of grace," because his influence was so great in this area.

Augustine's theology of grace grew out of his own experience of utter impotence and helplessness before God. In his famous autobiography, *The Confessions,* Augustine described his struggle and failure to live a life pleasing to God:

> No restraint was imposed by the exchange of mind with mind. . . . Clouds of muddy carnal concupiscence filled the air. The bubbling impulses of puberty befogged and obscured my heart so that it could not see the difference between love's serenity and lust's darkness. Confusion of the two things boiled within me . . . sweeping me through the precipitous rocks of desire to submerge me in a whirlpool of vice. . . . I was tossed about and split, scattered and boiled dry in my fornications. And you were silent. . . . I attribute to your grace and mercy that you have melted my sins away like ice.[3]

In his search for peace, Augustine tried many religions and schools of thoughts. For several years he was a follower of Manichaeanism, a fatalistic religion based on radical dualism: light and darkness, good and evil locked together forever in a great cosmic battle. Then he became a skeptic, a philosophy that denied the possibility of absolute truth. His conversion to Christ occurred as he was sitting in a garden reading a passage from Romans 13. In that moment he realized that his self-striving was useless and would never lead him to God. By God's grace he resolved to "put on the Lord Jesus Christ." Then immediately, he said, "the light of certainty flooded my heart and all dark shadows of doubt fled away."

Augustine rediscovered what Paul had proclaimed: Apart from the grace of Christ we are hopelessly lost and can do nothing to save ourselves. Yet this emphasis runs counter to the prevailing spirit of the age in which we live. That spirit is well expressed in the following verse, entitled "Determination," found inscribed on a box of tea at the grocery store:

> Gifts count for nothing; will alone is great;
> All things give way before it, soon or late. . . .
> Each well-born soul must win what it deserves. . . .
> The fortunate is he whose earnest purpose never swerves,
> Whose slightest action or inaction serves
> The one great aim.
> Why, even Death stands still,
> And waits an hour sometimes for such a will.

This is what the culture of self-reliance has taught us all. Gifts count for nothing. What does count is your will, your determination. You can make it on your own. Grace is for weaklings. You need no Savior to die for you, because you can save yourself by what you do and how you live. Just dig in deeper and try harder! William Ernest Henley's famous poem "Invictus" expresses the same idea in its exaltation of "my unconquerable soul." The would-be conqueror declares, "I am the master of my fate: I am the captain of my soul."

Much of the problem at Corinth stemmed from the fact that this kind of philosophy of life had made inroads into the Christian community there. Paul writes to remind them that self-salvation is an impossibility. Life itself is a gift. Moment by moment we are sustained by God's gracious providence. Everything we are and have is the result of our dependence on God's mercy. He brings these thoughts together in one verse: 1 Corinthians 4:7. This verse was also a favorite text of Augustine in his struggles with Pelagius. It consists of three questions: (1) Who makes you different from anyone else? (2) What do you have that you did not receive? (3) And if you did receive it, why do you boast as though you did not?

When they reflect on it, all Christians know that God did not save them because they are better, or smarter, or nicer looking than anyone else. In the Old Testament, God reminded the children of Israel that He had not chosen them because they were large in number, or mighty in battle, or rich in resources. No, they were at the very bottom of the "most-favored-nation" list. Why, then, did God choose Israel? Because He loved them—just because! And what can any of us claim to have, to possess, that we have not received as a gift? The honest answer has to be . . . nothing, nothing at all. The air we breathe, the clothes we wear, the food we eat, our families, our jobs, our friends, our faith: All of this has come to us as a gift from our gracious God (cf. James 1:17). Because this is true, there is no basis for boasting in the Christian life, no room for one-upmanship in the family of God. In the realm of grace, we lose all our bragging rights. Here we can only glory, as Paul said, "in the cross of our Lord Jesus Christ" (Galatians 6:14).

Most evangelicals have grown up with the language of grace and the music of grace, but sometimes our hearts have grown hardened to the true reality of grace. We suffer from grace-inflation. God's love and mercy no longer amaze, astound, and shatter. But once we understand who God is and what He has done for us in Jesus Christ, we will see that God's grace is an active, life-changing reality. The more we see our own unworthiness, the more astounded we are at God's gracious favor and mercy toward us. And the more we realize that our life purpose must be to glorify God, to please Him in every way, the more others will notice the results of God's transforming grace in our lives. When this happens, the world will see in us the mark of the Christian.

Loving Your Neighbor
When It Seems Impossible

In the 1980s, Lee Atwater, a high-ranking consultant for the National Republican Party, constituted the ultimate political attack dog. He exhibited a "take no prisoners" attitude. He focused on ruining his enemies' reputations. He specialized in planting bogus and demeaning stories in the media that would portray his foes in a very unflattering light.

Then, at the height of his political influence, Atwater was stricken by a grave disease. An evangelical Christian in Washington, D.C., witnessed to him about Jesus Christ. Atwater confessed his faith in Christ, even doing so publicly at a presidential prayer breakfast.

Atwater later made some telephone calls and wrote a series of letters. But this time he had a different mission than attacking an opponent. He wanted to ask for forgiveness and reconciliation from the very individuals against whom he had played his infamous "dirty tricks."

Among the recipients of Atwater's apologies was a Democratic politician. Atwater had nearly ruined this politician's life by revealing an "episode" in the man's past. A remorseful Atwater asked the man for forgiveness: "It is very important to me that I let you know that out of everything that has happened in my career, one of the low points remains the so-called '. . . episode.'"

So moved was this Christian man by the apology, he attended Atwater's funeral. He later observed: "I hope those young political consultants who would emulate Atwater's tactics of driving up the negatives of their opponents with the politics of fear will realize that Lee Atwater, confronting death, became, through the grace of God, an advocate of the politics of love and reconciliation."

LOVING AT ALL COSTS

Both Lee Atwater and the Democratic politician demonstrated the kind of "seeable," costly love that Francis Schaeffer said non-Christians have the right to expect from us as believers. "We are to love all true Christian brothers in a way that the world may observe," Schaeffer wrote. "This means showing love to our brothers in the midst of our differences—great or small—loving our brothers when it costs us something, loving them even under times of tremendous emotional tension, loving them in a way the world can see. . . . Love—and the unity it attests to— is the mark Christ gave Christians to *wear* before the world. Only with this mark may the world know that Christians are indeed Christians and Jesus was sent by the Father."[1]

Why was Francis Schaeffer so convinced that loving our brothers and sisters in Christ demonstrates we are true believers and helps the world know that Jesus was sent by the Father? Schaeffer understood this is what our Lord explicitly taught.

Schaeffer noted that "in John 13 and 17, Jesus talks about a real seeable oneness, a practicing oneness, a practical oneness across all lines, among all true Christians." He called on believers to "show a *practical* demonstration of love in the midst of the dilemma even when it is costly."[2]

Jesus put the matter as a command: "A new commandment I give you: Love one another. As I have loved you, so you must love one another. All men will know that you are my disciples if you love one another" (John 13:34–35). Elsewhere Jesus said: "My prayer is not for them alone. I pray also for those who will believe in me through their message, that all of them may be one, Father, just as you are in me and I am in you. . . . May they be brought to complete unity to let the world know that you sent me and have loved them as you have loved me" (John 17:20–21, 23).

Despite the clear teaching of Jesus, this kind of love is often in short supply. It can be a scarce commodity in our very own families. It may also be elusive in our church families. Many of us agree with Francis Schaeffer that "seeable . . . costly" love is what the Lord expects from us. We may doubt, however, whether we personally have the inner strength to demonstrate this kind of love. The cost of seeking reconciliation with those "certain" Christians we really do not like may seem just too exorbitant. Given the hurts we think they have inflicted upon us, we cannot imagine any circumstances in which we would risk seeking reconciliation with them.

We recognize that loving another person generally costs us something—especially our time, our emotional energy, and our material resources. We bear these costs much more easily if we believe the person likes or loves us. Indeed, we are drawn to people who reciprocate our good feelings toward them. Do they not want our best? Do they not speak well of us? Do they not try to console or encourage us when we are feeling bad? Do they not seem to listen to us?

By contrast, for us to contemplate loving persons who have wronged us, that is another matter.

WHY WE HESITATE TO RECONCILE

Multiple reasons may help explain our hesitancy to seek reconciliation:

1. We may assume that these "other" Christians would have little interest in seeking reconciliation with us. Why, then, should we initiate any special effort to reach out to them?

2. We may think that certain people will interpret any effort we make at reconciliation as a sign of our weakness. They would blame us, never say they are sorry, and never offer any gesture of restitution. Rather, we speculate, they will use our talk of reconciliation as a warrant to tell others they were in the right all along.

3. We may fear attempting to talk out our differences with an individual who is more verbally skillful than we are. This person knows just the way to make us feel bad. We may view this "other" Christian as an individual who always has to be right. They make pronouncements on everything—what is the right kind of church music, the right kind of preaching, the right meaning of a scriptural text, and so forth. When someone dares to disagree with this person, the individual explodes and puts the dissenter down in excited, abusive speech. We know this, for on several occasions, the person has put *us* down. Is it not understandable why we have little appetite for seeking reconciliation with this person? We set up boundaries and create space for ourselves as a survival tactic, to shield us from their incoming verbal missiles.

4. We may feel insufficiently trained in counseling to come along some persons. We may have surmised that these people engage in hurting others because they are hurting. We may not see ourselves as skilled Christian counselors. Nor do we have the emotional energy, nor the insights to try to minister to these persons.

5. We may have "reconciliation fatigue." We may have given up on attempting to improve relations with certain people. Talk of "reconciliation" makes us feel numb. We are tired of it.

6. We may sense that we are in part responsible for the estrangement that has emerged between ourselves and the other person. We may hesitate to admit this and to say that we are sorry and ask for forgiveness.

Any of these reasons can justify our hesitancy regarding seeking reconciliation. That burden seems simply too much for us to bear in certain instances. Indeed, respected Christian counselors may have told us it is. Or they may have suggested to us that we should put off seeking reconciliation until conditions are more suitable for such an initiative. Or they may have urged us to overlook the slights and faults of the other person.

With this "forgive and forget strategy" we might forgive the person even if we do not speak directly with him or her. The individual may never know we had an issue with them that caused us great discomfort.

Yet Francis Schaeffer's admonition that Christians should demonstrate *seeable* and *costly* love for other Christians will not go away. It challenges us.

How to *Truly* Forgive

What to do? A number of steps might be considered. *First,* we may wish to *determine if the reasons for our hesitancy to seek reconciliation with someone else are legitimate* or if they constitute excuses. *Second,* we may wish to *read insightful studies* on true forgiveness. D. A. Carson and Lewis Smedes, among others, have commented on the nature of biblical love and forgiveness. Regarding forgiveness, Smedes wrote: "Forgiving is the only way to heal the wounds of a past we cannot change and cannot forget. . . . Forgiving happens in three stages. We discover the humanity of the person who wronged us, we surrender our right to get even, and we wish that person well."[3]

In this light, we may seek to understand the dispute from the other party's point of view. They may be facing difficult and extenuating circumstances in life of which we did not have knowledge. These circumstances may help explain why they treat us the way they do.

Third, we would do well to *turn over whatever wrong they committed against us to the Lord* for His judgment. After all, each one of us will give an account of our own lives to the Lord at His judgment seat (Romans 14:10–12): "Why do you judge your brother? Or why do you look down on your brother? For we will all stand before God's judgment seat. It is written: '"As surely as I live," says the Lord, "every knee will bow before me; every tongue will confess to God."' So then, each of us will give an account of himself to God." For example, abuse victims often make their greatest advances in dealing with their anger and hurts when they give over what happened to God and remember that He knows very well what did happen. They do not have to try and settle up accounts by striking back at the abuser.

Fourth, we may *ask the Lord for the strength to love and forgive the Christians in question.*

Fifth, with the advice of trusted counselors, *we might attempt to draw up specific action steps* to take in seeking reconciliation. Anywhere along the line, a trusted Christian friend or counselor may suggest to us that we hold back from seeking reconciliation for apparently legitimate reasons.

Many Christians have faced the same reconciliation struggles we confront. Some of them believed they should evidence *seeable, costly* love and yet felt incapable of doing so. They too worried that the other party might reject their overtures, refuse to make restitution, and resort to scornful rebukes. They knew that their attempt at seeking reconciliation might fail (although their consciences might be cleared for making the effort). Despite fears that seeking reconciliation might even make things worse, some proceeded forward in this enterprise. We might find encouragement and inspiration by reviewing a number of their stories.

THE HIGH COST OF
REMAINING AT ODDS

Most of us have a fairly accurate idea of the substantial cost of seeking reconciliation with people we really do not like. And we may conclude the cost is too high. However, we may not have calculated the high cost of continuing to maintain our estrangement from these same Christians. When members of a family are angry with each other, no amount of money and good standing in the community can compensate for the deep sense of loss and pain experienced by family members. A mother and a father may seek a divorce, children can feel betrayed by their parents and siblings, visitors to the home can sense the icy coldness with which family members treat one another. Often the offended family members carry with them deep wounds—the source of their anger, frustration, and vengeful thoughts.

Likewise, in the church family, when members are at odds with each other, their desire to worship God together, to pray together, and to support common causes for Christ diminishes greatly. This does not mean individuals cannot be used of God when they find themselves in fractured relations. It does suggest that if disunity prevails in a family or in a church family, the Christians' witness to non-Christians will often diminish greatly. Many unbelievers will have a very difficult time recognizing Christians as Christ's authentic disciples if they see believers at each others' throats or coldly spurning each other's company.

Moreover, as Jonathan Edwards noted, spiritual pride, which is often the culprit in these matters, clogs the work of the Holy Spirit in a church. Such pride is evident when people have a judgmental spirit toward others, do not esteem others as better than themselves, and refuse to humble themselves and seek reconciliation. With remarkable insight Edwards describes how spiritual pride manifests itself:

> Spiritual pride disposes to speak of other persons' sins, their enmity against God and his people, the miserable delusion of hypocrites and their enmity against vital piety, and the deadness of some saints, with bitterness, or with laughter and levity, and an air of contempt; whereas pure Christian humility rather disposes, either to be silent about them, or to speak of them with grief and pity. . . . Spiritual pride is very apt to suspect others, whereas a humble saint is most jealous of himself; he is so suspicious of nothing in the world as he is of his own heart. The spiritually proud person is apt to find fault with other saints, that they are low in grace, and to be much in observing how cold and dead they be, and crying out of them for it; and to be quick to discern and notice of their deficiencies; but the eminently humble Christian has so much to do at home, and sees so much evil in his own heart, and is so concerned about it, that he is not apt to be very busy with others' hearts; he complains most of himself, and cries out of his own coldness and lowness in grace, and is apt to esteem others better than himself.[4]

In Ephesians 4:2–3, Paul calls us to interact with one another in a gentle, humble fashion: "Be completely humble and gentle; be patient, bearing with one another in love. Make every effort to keep the unity of the Spirit through the bond of peace."

Reconciliation is powerful; genuine reconciliation in a family may even spark a far-reaching spiritual revival.

The Western Canadian Revival of 1971 provides an instructive illustration of how the reconciliation of the members of a particular family helped spark a revival in a local church family that in turn spread to other churches and elsewhere in provinces of Western Canada and even to corners of the United States. In his own words, Pastor Ken Klassen of Regina, Saskatchewan, Canada, recounts the story he knows well. It means much to him. The reconciliation took place between his two uncles and led to the conversion of his father.

The story is "carefully researched," Klassen reports, and "collaborated by interviews with the surviving widows, brother, and the pastor and elder who were present. This is a story of reconciliation sparking revival."

On the first night of a scheduled ten-day revival crusade (October 13, 1971), approximately 165 people attended. Each meeting had a simple service structure: some singing, concise yet candid sermons, and several testimonies from laypeople from two Canadian provinces to the west.

The laypeople that night testified of God's grace and the overwhelming conviction of the Holy Spirit. No one responded to an invitation at the end of the message. Klassen describes what happened the next night:[5]

"The second night witnessed my aunt respond to God's finger pointing piercingly at her heart. Although a highly committed believer and even a recruited counselor for this crusade, she found herself before God at the altar a broken person in need of reconciliation. Leaving the altar with radiant joy, she no longer waited for others to apologize. She now took the initiative and asked for their forgiveness. But this was only the tip of the iceberg that would melt under the intense revival flame that was about to be ignited.

"Four days passed before brokenness and humility would force two brothers, my uncles, to face each other and resolve their conflict. A visitor sensitized by the Holy Spirit discerned that there was an unresolved conflict that was hindering the work of God. The pastor was aware of the tension between the two brothers.

"The thirteen-year estrangement now exhibited itself in a two-year breakdown in communication between them. To the outsider it was perceived as a feud, but to an insider it was a clash of two very strong but different personalities. A series of small differences and misunderstandings built up over the years until bitterness took root (Ephesians 4:31; Hebrews 12:15).

"The persuasive and compelling stories of transformed lives were the Spirit's medicine that would eventually bring healing and restoration to the brothers," Klassen recalls. "The older brother's heart would melt first. Counseled to pursue reconciliation with his brother, the older brother wrestled with past failed attempts. He knew his brother would be reluctant. More stories from the visitors who had experienced the healing and restoring power of revival poured salt into the open wound. It was if they had 'insider' information on the younger brother's life of dysfunction.

"In fact, he was convinced that his sister asked the visitors to talk to him. Infuriated, he wrote a letter to his sister in which he accused her of complicity: 'What's the big idea telling those men all about me so they could figure out just what to say to hit me?' His sister's responding letter was used by the Spirit to melt his bitter cold heart. She informed him that she didn't know anything about the visitors going to his church. The younger brother was slowly realizing that God's hand was pressing heavily on his shoulders."

The following Monday evening the pastor asked the church moderator (who was also a deacon) to join him in confronting the brothers. The two leaders invited the brothers to a Sunday school room in the church basement. There the older brother humbly entreated, "Forgive me, my brother." The younger answered haughtily, "It's about time you came!"

The older brother was crestfallen. He turned to the pastor and said, "You see, I knew he wouldn't forgive me." He turned to leave. Klassen describes what happened next.

"The pastor immediately prayed, 'Lord, don't let him go!' The man stopped, bowed his head, and just stood there. The pastor tried to talk to the younger brother, but the brother seemed to be more hardened than ever. The pastor and deacon began to pray again.

"Then the younger brother broke down and for twenty-five minutes cried to God for mercy. Human cries for mercy and pounding on a classroom wall resonated in the basement. After about a half hour, the four emerged from downstairs. Before the assembled crowd, the brothers testified of the wonderful work of God's grace in reconciliation. The families of the brothers converged at the front, hugging and kissing, dancing and laughing.

"With people getting right with God and with one another the barriers that had prevented the revival flame from igniting were vanquished. There was such contrition and brokenness that people forgot about the clock. The reconciliation would extend to the younger brother resolving conflict with a church he and his family had left some years before. The news of the reconciliation would bring my own father to saving knowledge of Jesus Christ, although he had fooled others for years, including himself."

After the reconciliation of the brothers in the church basement, the revival appeared to gain great strength. A letter to the editor of a local newspaper (24 November 1971) described well its impact upon the local community. Among its excerpts:

We have had many evangelistic crusades in Saskatoon. Through the years many have got right with God and have proved the reality of this by their lives, which are changed for good. But in these days something even greater is happening. People are getting right with one another, as well.

Hundreds of Christians are publicly and privately making old wrongs right: grudges of years standing have melted away. Restitution is being made by many who have stolen or cheated, as many businesses can testify. Men, who had cheated others in business deals have, in these days, felt the need to reimburse the wrong.

Bitterness and hate are melting away. Family fights are being breached and marital problems solved. Young people, hitherto involved in the drug habit, are being completely delivered from it.

The phenomenon of all this, is that these things are happening in many churches in the city, in the province, and . . . other western provinces at the same time.

The letter to the editor concluded with this telling paragraph:

For so long we have heard the complaint there are so many hypocrites in the churches. This has certainly been true. I know, however, many who read this will find themselves with a kinder neighbor, a more faithful employee, or a more understanding employer, as a result of what has been happening in our city during these last four weeks.[6]

Pastor Klassen indicated that following their reconciliation, "the brothers sang duets and shared their testimonies. . . . Their marriages and family life were rekindled and renewed." Other reconciled Christians began to bear the mark of the Christian in a seeable, costly way. Non-Christians were able to see in the actions and demeanor of these believers that they were Christ's disciples. Through the power of the Holy Spirit, these Christians had forsaken their sins, made restitution, and gained the capacity to love their neighbors in ways previously thought impossible.

Some years later, Erwin Lutzer wrote *Flames of Freedom* (1976), a marvelous account of the revival that affected his own family as well. In fact, Dr. Lutzer's brother, Harold Lutzer, cofounded the Canadian Revival Fellowship in 1972. The ministry continues to seek reconciliation between people within a given church before it helps them with evangelistic outreach programs.

Pastor Klassen's uncles had risked much in facing each other in a Sunday school room of the basement of a church. They began to talk with each other despite their very real fears that the costs of doing so were too much to bear. In a similar fashion, we need to seek reconciliation even when the costs seem more than we can handle. Though there are risks, we will not be alone. The Holy Spirit can give us the strength to do what we now believe is impossible. And caring friends may give us wise counsel or help mediate the reconciliation process.

The cost of maintaining estrangement from other believers is often far higher than any cost we might pay in seeking reconciliation. Not to resolve personal conflicts can hinder the Holy Spirit's work in our life and in the lives of others. Moreover, when reconciliation among Christians does take place, spiritual revival or renewal often follows.

RECONCILIATION AND RACE

The son of Christian Korean immigrants, Peter Cha grew up in a central Los Angeles community that was predominantly African-American. By his own account, his youth was miserable. Thinking that Peter knew kung fu, his classmates baited him to fight: "Hey, man, do you know kung fu?" On occasions he fought. His classmates taunted him.

Not knowing English very well, Peter had few friends. He felt very lonely. He emerged from his experience in L.A. with unresolved feelings of racial prejudice and conflict particularly toward African-Americans. He completed studies at the University of Chicago and Trinity Evangelical Divinity School and then joined the staff of InterVarsity Christian Fellowship. But his feelings of alienation toward African-Americans remained.

When the L.A. riots broke out in April 1992, Peter Cha filled with anger, especially after reading accounts of Korean-American store owners killed and injured in L.A. But in his devotions, he was also reading the beginning chapters of Isaiah, where God rebuked the children of God for their lack of concern for justice and the care for the poor.

Under deep conviction, Peter confessed his sinful attitude of hostility toward African-Americans and began to work for racial reconciliation in the name of Christ. Members of the InterVarsity leadership staff were coming to similar convictions during this time. They asked Peter to speak to the 1993 InterVarsity Conference at the University of Illinois, Urbana.

God used Peter Cha's address to a large plenary session of the conference in marvelous ways. Cha later explained that his message was to "passionately [exhort] that all people of God in North America be reconciled through Christ, so that the unity displayed could witness to the power and beauty of the Gospel of Jesus Christ." He was unaware that two hundred delegates from Japan, part of a larger contingent of 470 international students at the conference, heard this call for reconciliation and were willing to make an immediate application.

When the nearly five hundred delegates representing sixty-eight nations gathered for an international student conference at the end of the historic mission convention, the Japanese Christian students gathered each evening to pray for the ministry of the Gospel in their nation.

In an account prepared for this book, Cha explained what happened as they prayed:

> Each time they met, God challenged them to continue to wrestle with the mandate of reconciliation. Specifically, they felt called to repent for the sins their nation committed against other Asian nations during the first half of the twentieth century, the very act their government was fiercely refusing to carry out at the time.
>
> Then one evening, they invited Korean delegates to their prayer meeting, asking for their forgiveness as they confessed the sins of their own nation. In response, the Korean delegates, weeping, began to repent for their hardened hearts for not forgiving Japan in the past. The evening prayer meeting continued until five in the morning as they prayed for one another, as they began to put an end to the longstanding hostility that existed between the two people groups. The prayer meeting ended with Korean student leaders singing a hymn of blessing to their Japanese brothers and sisters, with their hands opened and reaching out to the Japanese delegates, while the latter knelt down on the floor with their hands stretched out to receive this blessing from their Korean brothers and sisters. Tears of joy streamed down their faces as they realized the wall between them was completely taken away and there were no longer obstacles to stop them from enjoying and loving one another. How amazing the power of reconciliation!
>
> The next morning, during the general assembly session, the Japanese delegation decided to express this new reality in a very public way. When

one of the Japanese leaders came to the platform, all of the Japanese students stood and lined the walls of the auditorium as their leader publicly confessed the sins of their nation. They then bowed to the ground with their faces to the floor before the audience, to express their genuine sorrow and contriteness. The next day, the Korean delegates who were scheduled to lead worship, took the opportunity to acknowledge the Japanese expression of humility and love, and to express their own forgiveness of the Japanese. They, in turn, then asked for forgiveness for the sins of the Korean people. Delegates from all over the world who witnessed these public acts of reconciliation were deeply moved, taking this invaluable lesson back to their nations.[7]

Students from the two countries put their forgiveness into action, deciding to form a new missions group called Japanese and Korean Fellowship to further promote reconciliation between these two people groups and to create a new partnership in the ministry of evangelism in Japan.

Cha concluded, "Their experience, thus, illustrates the biblical principle that our reconciliation with God and our reconciliation with 'others' must continually reinforce and energize one another."

His story reminds us that racial conflicts can take place between various ethnic groups and that, through the power of the Holy Spirit, reconciliation can take place between these same peoples. At the same time, Cha could have never spoken the way he did unless he had personally experienced the Holy Spirit's power to help him repent of his own unresolved racial animosities.

Today, many Christians of different ethnic and racial backgrounds are extending love across racial lines. If the evangelical community at large would do this, non-Christians would be able to recognize more easily that we bear the mark of a Christian.

THE CHANGING CONTOUR
OF THE PROBLEM OF RACE

Some politicians, educators, social workers, and law enforcement officers worry that charged racial and ethnic relations could become a tinderbox igniting societal unrest in the United States deep into the twenty-first century. In terms of sheer demographics, some are describing a "new racial paradigm" emerging in the United States. In a column in the *Chicago Tribune,* Clarence Page unpacks a significant trait of this paradigm: "By mid-century, demographers project the entire country's population could become like California, where the census says, minorities became the majority in 1999." In 2002, the U.S. Hispanic population (13.4 percent) surpassed the African-American population (13.1 percent). By 2050, the number of Hispanics will triple, and Asian-Americans will represent 8 percent of the population.[8]

Whereas African-Americans and Hispanics may have issues with Anglos, they also have grievances with each other. Page cites political turf protection and feuds that have sprung up between Hispanics and African-Americans. Peter Cha's story makes it clear that in large cities relations are not always peaceful between Asian-Americans and African-Americans. Then again, white Americans may become more anxious and resentful as they continue to lose a dominant role, at least numberswise, in the society at large. Radical white supremacists who resort to violence exist in considerable numbers.

In *The Problem of Race in the 21st Century,* historian Thomas Holt has argued that the Fordist era (named after Henry Ford's famed assembly line for manufacturing) brought African-Americans into the auto industry with stable wages and benefits and union protection, only to yield in the late 1960s to a decentralized workplace, as large American corporations turned to cheap labor in the Caribbean and Southeast Asia. Many manufacturing jobs in the United States were eliminated, with major savings of up to 40 percent in production costs.

Along with other ethnic groups, many African-Americans lost the relatively good jobs they had due to this "outsourcing." Often any new jobs created in the transition were low paying and in the service sector. Meanwhile, white businesspeople frequently networked with other whites in hiring of personnel to manage corporations in the expanding new global economy.

Taking into consideration the massive changes in the job market brought on by the post-Fordist era, Holt argues that it is insufficient to understand racism in terms of older definitions: "the hostility one group feels toward another on the basis of the alleged biological and/or cultural inferiority of that other." Rather the "problem of race" is now much more complex. For one thing, Holt and a number of other scholars contend that race is socially constructed and not biologically determined. For another, Holt believes present-day racism is linked to the seismic economic shifts of post-Fordist America—shifts from which African-Americans did not generally benefit. Holt writes: "Despite the dramatic rise in the number of middle-income blacks and, by historical measures, their visible integration into major institutions of the national life, one of the clearest consequences of the transformed economy has been the massive exclusion of blacks from the *formal* economy. And with that exclusion comes the loss of a standard of living and social securities envisaged for industrial workers under a Fordist regime."[9]

Holt is not convinced that major economic and governmental institutions have the will to redress the inequalities and injustices emerging in the new economic order. Holt and other writers help us to understand better the racism that continues to bedevil our society in ways Christians may not have recognized or anticipated. At the same time, these writings may discourage us once we grasp the amplitude of the problem. They may cause us to wonder if there is anything we can do to challenge racism in a way that might make a difference.

EVANGELICALS AND THE PROBLEM OF RACE

Whatever our ethnic or racial background, most of us as evangelical Christians know that racism in its various forms is totally alien to Christ's teaching that we are to love our neighbors as ourselves. But discerning as individuals what our specific response should be is often difficult for us to do. Most of us do not have access to the levers of power that affect the structures of government and law enforcement, the policies of corporate commercial entities, and the admission policies of educational institutions. After reading studies by Holt and others that focus on the institutional basis of racism, we may think there is relatively little we can undertake to make changes at the societal level.

At the same time, "the problem of race" may constitute a remarkable opportunity for us to bear the mark of Jesus before a watching world—displaying love toward all believers, whatever their ethnic or racial background. Andrew Walls, a distinguished missiologist, notes that due to America's generous immigration law of the 1960s, "nearly all the main Christian discourses have functioning congregations [in America]. More than in any other nation in the world, the body of Christ could be realized—or fractured—in the United States."[10]

Enhancing this opportunity even further is R. Stephen Warner's remarkable finding that two-thirds of the new immigrants arriving in the United States view themselves as Christians. In a recent *Christian Century* article Warner observes: "Above all, the new immigrants make it decreasingly plausible for Americans to think of Christianity as a white person's religion."[11] Among Protestant immigrants, the majority are Pentecostals and evangelicals. In reaching out across racial and ethnic lines, we may find among the new immigrants people who would welcome our initiative in the name of Christ.

To maximize the opportunity to which Andrew Walls alludes, evangelicals might consider addressing the problem of race on two fronts. Those evangelicals who are in a position to bring about structural changes in American institutional life that would promote greater justice and economic equality for all races should attempt to do so. Those who have no such power should attempt to improve relations with people of other ethnic and racial backgrounds in their own, more limited spheres of influence.

In truth, often in the past we have not been exemplary in putting those teachings into practice. We may be much more interested in supporting foreign missions than getting to know Christians of other races across town. In fact, the larger world does not generally perceive us (with the notable exception of certain churches and parachurch groups like Promise Keepers and Prison Fellowship) as at the forefront of efforts of racial reconciliation. Rather conservative Christians are often deemed promoters of segregation and racism. Significant literature exists making this explicit point.

Things have not changed greatly in the forty years since Martin Luther King wrote his *Letter from a Birmingham Jail* (1963), which described poignantly the silence of "the contemporary church" regarding social injustices including segregation:

> So often the contemporary church is a weak, ineffectual voice with an uncertain sound. So often it is an arch defender of the status quo. Far from being disturbed by the presence of the church, the power structure of the average community is consoled by the church's silent—and often very vocal—sanction of things as they are. But the judgment of God is upon the church as never before. If today's church does not recapture the sacrificial spirit of the early church, it will lose its authenticity, forfeit the loyalty of millions, and be dismissed as an irrelevant social club with no meaning for the twentieth century.

On the fortieth anniversary (2003) of its publication, a number of columnists for American newspapers quoted this passage as still an accurate portrayal of many of the nation's churches.

In *Divided by Faith: Evangelical Religion and the Problem of Race in America* (Oxford Univ. Press, 2000), authors Michael Emerson and Christian Smith specifically chastise white evangelical Christians for their alleged complicity in upholding the "racial divide" in the United States, arguing that their reliance on interpersonal relationships and an "inability to perceive or unwillingness to accept social structural influences" perpetuate racial division and inequality.

Emerson and Smith also believe that when Christians rely on personal reconciliation with people of other "races" as the means to overcome the racial divide, they will not address the more substantive issue of the social structural forces that foster racism within American society. For them, the Christians' goals of personal conversion and reconciliation reflect the evangelicals' reliance on their tools "of accountable freewill individualism" and "relationalism."

SEEKING RECONCILIATION AMONG THE RACES

What should we make of this literature? We could dismiss it out of hand in a defensive fashion. For example, we could rightfully point out that Emerson and Smith underestimate the value of Christian interpersonal "relations" between individuals in bringing about reconciliation among the races. They do not appear to have categories for dealing with the work of the Spirit of God in bringing about the kind of racial reconciliation described in Peter Cha's story. Moreover, they place an unfair burden of guilt on most individual evangelicals by claiming the latter should bring about systemic changes in the social, economic, and governmental institutions in the United States when these same believers do not generally have direct access to the levers that would trigger these transformations.

At the same time, when their criticisms are accurate, we should accept them in a humble spirit. We can also gain insights about the nature of the "racial divide" in the United States from their analysis. We should take seriously their admonition to work toward change in those institutions that promote injustice and inequality.

Another reaction might be for us to succumb to "reconciliation fatigue." We could hunker down, deny the existence of "the problem of race," and totally ignore the issues raised in this literature.

If we were to adopt this last option, it would greatly restrict our capability of bearing the mark of Jesus before a watching world. It would be as if we forget Jesus' teaching that we are to love our neighbors as ourselves, whoever they are.

REMEMBERING WE BELONG TO ONE ANOTHER

Crawford Loritts, an African-American who speaks frequently for Campus Crusade and Promise Keepers, has wryly described our "predicament." He reminds us that "we are all stuck with each other" whether we like it or not. We are, after all, Christians first, then Asian-Americans, Hispanic-Americans, African-Americans, Indian-Americans and white-Americans.

As members of Christ's body, we belong to Christ and therefore to one another: "Just as each of us has one body with many members, and these members do not all have the same function, so in Christ we who are many form one body, and each member belongs to all the others" (Romans 12:4–5).

Sometimes our racial views blind us from recognizing this basic unity in Christ. We do not see that at the foot of the cross we are all on equal ground. We do not remember that we are all brothers and sisters in Christ.

Through the power of the Holy Spirit, however, all bitterness and negative feelings toward one another can be overcome. Many early Christians discovered the reality of this wonderful truth. Justin Martyr declared: "We who hated and killed one another and would not associate with men of different tribes because of [their different] customs, now after the manifestation of Christ live together and pray for our enemies and try to persuade those who unjustly hate us."

What happened in the early church can happen today. The same Holy Spirit who worked so powerfully in the early church can minister graciously to Christ's disciples and bring about racial reconciliation.

MORE "IMPOSSIBLE" STORIES
OF LOVING YOUR NEIGHBOR: SAMUEL'S STORY

An African-American man stood in the front of the classroom of about one hundred seminary students. Fifteen minutes before the class was to begin, the student had told the white professor (one of the present authors) how he had become a student at a largely white evangelical seminary. The teacher then asked the student to recount the story to his classmates, telling the class that he had invited their fellow student to begin the class session with his personal testimony.

A powerfully built man in his thirties, the African-American began to speak in a relaxed but measured fashion. His fellow students listened to every word. Samuel indicated that he had been raised in the housing projects of Chicago. He had never really spoken to a white person until he was almost eighteen. This did not mean he had no feelings about white people. He did. He hated them. He became a follower of a radical black separatist.

Samuel had gotten into trouble with the law and ended up in jail.

In prison someone gave him a Bible. He read about Jesus, he said. Then he made a statement that simply transfixed the students in the classroom: "And Jesus drained away all of my racism. That is why I can be with you white folks this evening."

Whatever the teacher taught that evening, the students probably do not remember. It is likely, however, that they remember this last statement from their fellow student: the power of Jesus Christ to heal a person's heart of racial prejudice, even bringing the individual (in accord with Jesus' teachings of Matthew 5:43–48) to the point of loving his former enemies.

DAVID AND JEFF'S STORY

A few years later, in another classroom setting and at the invitation of the professor, two African-Americans explained to other students the reasons they cared for white people. One of them, David Myles, had been raised in a predominantly white community. The other had been formerly a member of the Black Panthers, a radical militant group. They too said that Christ had healed their feelings of hurt and hatred regarding whites.

After the class, a number of students stayed around to talk further. Jeff Talbert, a white student, volunteered: "I was raised in an atheistic home. I became a Christian. But I must confess that I am afraid of you African-Americans."

With a smile on her face, an African-American woman replied: "Why are you afraid of me? When I became a Christian, I accepted Jesus' teaching that I was to love my neighbor, and I love you."

The two men first met during a small group discussion in their evangelism class. Later Myles and Talbert explained to the authors how the impossible had happened: They were reconciled to each other as brothers in Christ.

"Here was this blond-haired, blue-eyed white guy who had grown up on welfare and gone to Cameroon, Africa, as a missionary," David recalled. "He grew up in a broken home marred by abuse and divorce . . . compared with myself, an African-American who had grown up not on welfare and in a two-parent home." David felt shock when he learned Jeff had been an atheist before he came to Christ and had helped to found the Atheist Society of students at a West Coast university.

Meanwhile, Jeff was shocked by Dave's physical presence. "My first thought upon meeting Dave was, 'I wouldn't want to meet him in a dark alley.' He was tall, dark, and imposing, and I figured this was someone that I didn't want to get to know. I have never been more wrong about a first impression.

"The next week in our evangelism small group, Dave shared about helping someone who had car problems on the side of the road. As he walked toward the man, he realized that the sight of a strange, large black man might not be very welcome, so he flashed a big smile to ease the tension."

Jeff admitted that once he got beyond the exterior, he saw "a heart that loved Jesus and the people whom Jesus died for." He learned that Dave had grown up as one of the very few African-Americans in North Dakota and had endured constant racism. Yet one day Dave told him, "Jesus took the racism out of my heart."

"As he helped me to see the world through his eyes, I didn't like what I saw. I naively thought that white racism still lingered in small ways, but it was mostly a thing of the past. Dave showed me how constant and prevailing racism still is, and more powerfully, how much it hurt. A speaker we listened to described it as realizing that as an eight-year-old boy, most people just would rather you weren't around. As I got to know and love Dave, my protests of white guilt and how I was not a racist seemed pretty shallow. My friend was hurting; the least I could do was care."

"As our friendship grew, God started to show us the world through non-Christian eyes. We realized how hollow a segregated Christianity that focuses more on words and beliefs that are not lived out in love and service must appear to the world. God gave us a vision for a church that would bring all of God's people together from every tribe, tongue and nation [Revelation 7:9] to all worship and proclaim the same God.

"There is no way that blacks and whites or anyone else for that matter could come together in love and humbly serve one another unless the Holy Spirit was working in their midst. As God brought us together in this vision, we began to see that blacks and whites have gifts that the others lacked. We recognized how unbalanced we had become because the body of Christ was divided. We desperately needed each other to be complete as a church, to heal our wounds, and to glorify God before a doubting culture."

Through their vision Jeff and David have become more unified in their friendship. "Jeff's gentle heart and his authentic love for lost people impressed me," David noted. "Jeff had a desire to return to authentic Christianity and saw that racism and injustice grieved the heart of God. Here was a brother that I did not have to convince of the realities of racism and its evident sinfulness. He wanted to see Christ break the chains and shackles of the bondage of racism. I love Jeff and consider him a dear brother and would be honored to work with him."

The two now pray together and share the struggles in their lives. In this deepening friendship, Jeff admits being embarrassed by only one thing: "I'm embarrassed at my first impression, because today all I see is my close friend who loves the Lord so much. I've come to respect his advice about far more than understanding racism. He helps me with my relationship with God, my marriage, and the way I understand life. He's the first person I want to bounce ideas off of, not because he's black, but because he's my most trusted friend.

"God has taught me through my friendship with Dave things I could never learn through a book or class. God has shown me that African-Americans are people I care about, can learn from, and respect. There is no better way I know of wiping the scourge of racism from a human heart than a personal friendship like God has given me with Dave."

"Changing the Way I Think"

When David Myles and another African-American talked about Christ in the class, their words struck one white student deeply. The student, a pastor of a fairly large church, was moved by what he had heard. After the class, he volunteered to the teacher: "I have never been around African-Americans before. This was my first time. I had never heard my black brothers and sisters talk about their Christian faith before. This experience is changing the way I think."

This comment by the white student underscores the existence of the "racial divide" about which Emerson and Smith write. The "divide" often separates Christian believers of various ethnic or racial groups in the United States. We can literally live in two different worlds and have little knowledge of, or contact with, other ethnic and racial peoples who likewise belong to the body of Christ. We can be oblivious to the prejudice and social and economic inequalities these other Christians might face.

An African-American woman put the matter this way: "Why is it that white evangelical Christians just don't get it?" A successful businesswoman, she had become a Christian about five years earlier. By no means was she an embittered person. Nor was she caught up in a "victim's" mentality. She was simply exasperated. She could not understand how white evangelicals often seem to show little interest in the problems that their "other" brothers and sisters in Christ sometimes experience in this country. She also noted there were African-American Christians who showed little interest in the well-being of white evangelicals.

SHARING OUR LOVE WITH
THOSE OF OTHER RACES

If we are to demonstrate that we are Christ's disciples by the love we show one another, we need to come into contact with each other. Like David and Jeff, we need to care about each other's welfare. The apostle James asks: "Suppose a brother or sister is without clothes and daily food. If one of you says to him, 'Go, I wish you well; keep warm and well fed,' but does nothing about his physical needs, what good is it?" (James 2:15–16).

To some, this approach might appear simplistic. But for many of us, this is all we have to offer. We are neither governmental officials nor corporate heads nor educational leaders. Moreover, for some of us, moving out from our own comfort zones to care for people across racial and ethnic divides may indeed represent the costly, seeable love that Francis Schaeffer associated with the "mark of the Christian." Old ways of thinking about our own racial superiority or inferiority are not quickly abandoned. Old hurts do not quickly heal. Old suspicions do not always disappear overnight. But should we embrace this worthy enterprise of seeking reconciliation, we will not be alone. The Holy Spirit will be with us to give us power to do what we could not do on our own.

We might consider taking a few initial steps. *First, we can learn what these "other" Christians think about us.* We may be surprised by their perceptions. We may learn that some think we have little interest in them. We may discover that they believe aspects of what we deem authentic Christianity do not in fact square with their understanding of the Gospel. We need to listen carefully to their concerns.

Second, in a gracious spirit, *we can attempt to discern how these "other" Christians relate their faith to the world in which they live.* Church may play a greater role in their life experience than it does for us. They may emphasize the bearing of their faith upon issues like oppression, poverty, and social justice more than we do. They may remind us that the Bible says much about the importance of these matters.

Third, if these "other" Christians live nearby or "across town," *we can attempt to get to know them better on a personal basis.* In doing this, we would reach out and meet as equals, not as superiors, nor as inferiors. Some churches have bonded together as sister churches across racial lines. Their pastors meet from time to time, and their congregations sometimes hold joint services and activities. Other churches have ministries specifically oriented to various ethnic groups in the community. Still other churches are more fully racially integrated. Seeking the Lord's help in prayer is an essential element for any of these initiatives. They often demand from the participants displays of the costly, seeable love Francis Schaeffer describes as the "mark of the Christian."

Fourth, we can gain a more informed perspective on "other" Christians by reading books that focus on their respective cultural and social experiences. For insights on the Asian-American experience, read *Following Jesus Without Dishonoring Your Parents,* by Jeanette Yep, Peter Cha, and other Asian-American writers.[12] In *Being Latino in Christ,* Orlando Crespo provides insights on his experiences as a Hispanic believer and spells out his thoughts on racial reconciliation.[13]

In *The Anatomy of Racial Inequality,* Glenn C. Loury, an African-American, offers sobering data that confirm the discrepancy between the social and economic conditions many African-Americans encounter compared to those faced by white Americans.[14] Moreover, he affords a brilliant analysis of the origins of racial inequality in this country.

Before serving as university professor of economics and director of the Institute on Race and Social Divisions at Boston University, Loury was a tenured professor at Harvard University and one of the most well-respected economists and social commentators in the United States. And yet by his admission, his personal life was a mess. He was quite simply miserable. Then he found peace in Jesus Christ.

In *One by One from the Inside Out,* a book directed to a secular audience, Loury boldly inserted an epilogue entitled "New Life: A Professor and Veritas." He recounted how his life was completely changed after he accepted Christ as his Lord and Savior. His new found faith in Christ reshaped his thoughts on racial reconciliation and his practice of the social sciences:

> How do I know that the resurrection and the whole Gospel is real? I know not only because of an acquaintance with the primary sources from the first century A.D., or even because of the words of the Bible. I know primarily, and I affirm this truth to you, on the basis of what I have witnessed in my own life. This knowledge of God's unconditional love for humankind provides moral grounding for my work in cultural and racial reconciliation, economics, and social justice. Jesus Christ provides a basis for hope and for the most profound personal satisfaction. To paraphrase slightly a currently popular rallying cry: no Jesus, no peace.[15]

Loury helps us to understand some of the subtler forms of racism. He notes that the last thing many people want to be known as is a racist. Thus they will profess their support for the African-American community and for a color-blind society. At the same time, they may not really care about the actual welfare of African-Americans. Or an individual may applaud the fact that African-Americans have civil rights while simultaneously assuming that African-Americans are collectively inferior to whites in their skills. For example, if the person is in business and interviewing an African-American candidate for a job, he or she may pre-judge the candidate's capabilities due to the color of skin without taking the time to find out what skills the candidate actually possesses. Or a "liberal" social scientist, while ignoring the experience of millions of successful African-Americans, may portray the institutional sources of racism as so overpowering that African-Americans are made to look as if they have not even a hypothetical possibility of escaping difficult social and economic conditions through self-reliance.

For Loury, these are some of the forms of racism that, even if subtle, rob African-Americans of their dignity and worth.

READY TO RECONCILE?

The apostle Paul instructs us concerning what our demeanor should be in seeking reconciliation: "Be completely humble and gentle; be patient, bearing with one another in love. Make every effort to keep the unity of the Spirit through the bond of peace" (Ephesians 4:2–3).

Reconciliation brings great joy and peace to our souls. The wilderness time of painful estrangement and sadness comes to an end. With reconciliation, forgiveness replaces vengeful thoughts. Hurts begin to heal. A new freedom to worship and pray together emerges. A genuine desire to see good things happen to the other party is born. A watching world sees more clearly the unity of the body of Christ.

Once our fellowship with another brother or sister in Christ has been restored, we often wonder why we waited so long to seek reconciliation. And yet we probably know the answer to our own question. We had believed that the costs of seeking reconciliation were too exorbitant, the task simply impossible. We hesitated to take a first step.

But then we discovered that what we had reckoned unthinkable—loving a particular neighbor—did in fact happen. Amazingly enough, we were now reconciled with a brother or sister in Christ. We could warmly greet this individual who in earlier days we had tried to avoid or whose very presence had made us feel very uncomfortable. Moreover, we gratefully acknowledged that it was the power of the Holy Spirit that permitted this reconciliation. It was certainly not our own.

This certainly was the case when Lee Atwater, facing death, decided to make things right with people. Nonbelievers took notice and saw costly and observable love.

We should not wait until dire circumstances overtake us before seeking reconciliation with others. Reconciliation brings great peace to our souls when we engage in the "ministry of reconciliation" (2 Corinthians 5:18).

Obeying Christ's admonition to love our neighbors as ourselves also brings great joy and spiritual renewal, not only to us but to our families and our churches. And undoubtedly, it affords nonbelievers with the kind of evidence they need to have if they are to recognize in us the "mark of Jesus."

Evangelical Unity

Drawing
Boundaries and
Crossing Barriers

As we have seen, one mark of Jesus is to love our neighbors as ourselves. Our neighbors are all of our fellow human beings who share with us the habitation of the earth, Jesus said—even our enemies (Matthew 5:43–48; Luke 10:29–37). But another mark of Jesus strikes closer to home. We are to love deeply our fellow brothers and sisters in Christ.

Clearly, this is what Jesus had in mind as He gave this special instruction to His disciples on His way to the cross: "A new command I give you: Love one another. As I have loved you, so you must love one another. By this all men will know that you are my disciples, if you love one another" (John 13:34–35).

Although as followers of Jesus we are called upon to love all persons as our neighbors, indeed to love them as ourselves (Luke 10:27), there is a special obligation and a particular promise related to Jesus' "new command" in John 13. As Francis Schaeffer reminded us in *The Mark of the Christian*, Jesus here gives the world the right to decide whether we are true Christians based upon our observable love for one another. Yet since Jesus' ascension, Christians have divided on several issues—they remain divided on certain issues today.

QUESTIONS WE MUST ANSWER

These divisions give rise to several questions: What role does doctrine play in defining these differences? How can we be faithful to the truth of Scripture and still exhibit the mark of Jesus in our relationships with one another? Are all doctrinal differences the same? How can we distinguish issues on which we must take a stand—even if it means leaving the fellowship of a certain church—from other matters that, while important, should not be elevated to such a high level?

Each of the questions posed in the paragraph above can and indeed should be asked about the issue of Christian unity in general. While God alone is the ultimate judge of anyone's salvation, we believe that all those who truly trust in Jesus Christ as Savior and Lord are sons and daughters of God through grace, and hence are our brothers and sisters in Christ, regardless of their ecclesiastical tradition or denominational affiliation. We think it important for such believers to seek a greater unity in Jesus Christ, to talk honestly about the differences that still divide us into separated church groups and theological parties. It is also important to find ways of working together on matters of common interest, without violating our consciences, even as we acknowledge crucial differences that still remain between us. At the onset of this chapter, we state our belief about seeking unity among all of our fellow Christians: It is possible—and desirable—to pray and work for greater unity with our fellow believers even though we may not be able to achieve the complete unity we desire and still obviously lack.

We ourselves have been involved in such discussions, and much that we say in this chapter can be applied to the wider issue of Christian unity in general. However, our special focus here is on *evangelical unity*. We are not insensitive to the wider implications of this theme, but we have a particular burden for the evangelical church. Why? For two reasons: It is that part of the body of Christ to which we belong and in which we have been nurtured, called, and encouraged to serve the Lord in our own vocations. And second, we evangelicals are more often known for our divisions and mutual recriminations against one another than for our unifying efforts in evangelism and discipleship. We think this is a scandal that hinders the integrity of our witness before a watching world. We hope that what we say here will help evangelicals to think more clearly about expressing more convincingly, and more visibly, the unity we already share by God's grace as Bible-believing Christians so that the world may see and know that Jesus Christ is the way, the truth, and the life. This, we believe, is in keeping with the prayer Jesus offered to the heavenly Father as He prepared to go to the cross: "May they be brought to complete unity to let the world know that you sent me" (John 17:23).

WHY DOCTRINE MATTERS

In the early twentieth century, the emerging ecumenical movement emphasized the need to play down the importance of dogmatic beliefs and theological commitments among the churches because these were seen as hindrances to greater Christian cooperation in missions and evangelism. Ecumenical leaders who held this view invented the slogan "Doctrine Divides, Missions Unite." This view, and even this same slogan, can still be heard today among some well-meaning Christians who regard theology, or at least the taking of theology seriously, as a stumbling block to Christian togetherness.

Ironically, the maxim "Doctrine Divides, Missions Unite" can be heard from both sides of the theological spectrum. Several years ago, Konrad Reiser, then the general secretary of the World Council of Churches, called for a "paradigm shift" in the ecumenical movement. He called for an "urgent reordering of the ecumenical agenda away from old doctrinal disputes and unresolvable arguments of the past toward more urgent contemporary issues such as justice, peace, and concern for the environment."[1] According to this perspective, theological dialogue

among various Christian groups that hold historic differences on matters of faith and order in the life of the church has come to a dead end.
The folly of pursuing such "old doctrinal disputes" should be recognized
and abandoned in favor of a more urgent commitment to a liberal social agenda. Much of the mainline ecumenical movement has followed
Reiser's recommendation, and this is one reason official ecumenism has
lost so much of its earlier promise and momentum.

But a similar argument can be heard from some conservative evangelical Christians as well. Here doctrine tends to get downplayed as a
hindrance to the believer's ongoing relationship to Christ. Spirituality
is seen as a good thing, but theology is disparaged as an alien system of
ideas with little relevance to one's spiritual growth in Christ. Some evangelical models of church growth, fueled by the consumerist focus of
American culture, echo this same concern. The church, it is claimed,
should not impose doctrinal beliefs or behavioral requirements on anyone. The church, like a community center, exists to meet the needs of
those who use it, not to teach doctrine or make demands on its members. This idea was captured in an attractive, colorful sign outside a growing evangelical church in Kentucky: "The church that asks nothing of
you."

What is wrong with this perspective from a biblical point of view?
Simply put, it ignores the fact that it is impossible to divorce one's relationship with Christ—much less a commitment to the mission and ministry of His church—from a theological understanding of His person and
work. For example, when Paul said to the Thessalonian church, "For God
did not appoint us to suffer wrath but to receive salvation through our
Lord Jesus Christ" (1 Thessalonians 5:9), he was making a profound doctrinal claim about the One he believed could deliver those people from
their sins. "Christ" was not Jesus' last name, nor "Lord" His first! These
were both messianic titles fraught with rich theological meaning. The
essence of Christianity, according to the New Testament, is knowing and
trusting Jesus Christ, not in the abstract, but precisely as Lord, the incarnate Son of God, as Prophet, Priest, and King, as Savior, Redeemer,
and Victor.

To be sure, one can respond to Jesus in simple faith without exploring in depth all that these and other biblical ascriptions mean, just as the first disciples still had much to learn after they had obeyed the Master's command, "Come, follow Me." However, a major part of their preparation for future leadership was a matured understanding of who Jesus was and what He had come to do. Thus the earliest portrayal of the New Testament church depicts a band of committed believers who "devoted themselves to the *apostles' teaching*" (Acts 2:42, italics added).

In the church of the New Testament, doctrinal unity on the essentials of the gospel message was not only a requirement for leadership but also a test of fellowship. The Johannine community excluded as antichrist those proto-gnostics who denied the reality of the incarnation, although we know from the recently discovered Nag Hammadi writings that many of them claimed to have a personal "relationship with Christ." But this was a made-up Christ of their own concocted imaginings, not the Lord Jesus Christ of the four canonical Gospels.

Many popular presentations of Jesus today are no less off base. Whenever we hear Jesus presented as the answer to life's problems, or as a spiritual guru whose advice should be followed, we must always ask, "Whose Jesus?"; "Which Christ?" Jesus Himself warned about this danger: "Watch out that no one deceives you," He said. "For many will come in my name, claiming, 'I am the Christ,' and will deceive many" (Matthew 24:4–5).

This is why theology matters. We will not have the kind of spiritual discernment required for sorting through the many competing pathways of spirituality and Christology without a solid doctrinal foundation on which to stand.

United We Stand

Where do we find a foundation for the kind of doctrinal understanding that will keep us from lapsing into error or being deceived by pretender messiahs? Evangelicals believe that God has revealed His will to His people in the Holy Scriptures, which we accept as uniquely, verbally, and fully inspired by the Holy Spirit, even though the mode of the Bible's inspiration remains largely a mystery to us.

Over the years, evangelicals have issued many statements about the Bible, describing in slightly different ways its inspiration and authority. Here is what the Amsterdam Declaration (2000) says about the Bible: "The 66 books of the Old and New Testaments constitute the written Word of God. As the inspired revelation of God in writing, the Scriptures are totally true and trustworthy, and the only infallible rule of faith and practice. In every age and every place, this authoritative Bible, by the Spirit's power, is efficacious for salvation through its witness to Jesus Christ."

While the Bible remains the source, the content, and the criterion of all true theology, evangelicals have also generally recognized the historic creeds and confessions of the church as trustworthy summaries of scriptural teaching. To be sure, the Scriptures do not derive their authority from the church, tradition, or any other human source, yet we can recognize the heart of the Bible's message about Jesus Christ in such documents as the Apostles' Creed, the Nicene Creed, the various confessions and catechisms of the Reformation, as well as more recent evangelical doctrinal statements.

AN EVANGELICAL CONSENSUS

Three of the most important, and widely accepted, of these evangelical statements of faith are: The Lausanne Covenant (1974); "The Gospel of Jesus Christ: An Evangelical Celebration" (1999); and "The Amsterdam Declaration: A Charter for Evangelism in the Twenty-first Century" (2000). Using these three documents and other recent evangelical statements of faith, J. I. Packer and Thomas C. Oden have brought together in one volume what they call "the evangelical consensus," a common matrix of beliefs on major biblical and theological themes. In their recent book *One Faith: The Evangelical Consensus,* they argue that there is a coherent, underlying unity and solidarity among evangelicals; in other words, a theological coherence to be grasped in the various confessional-type documents evangelicals have produced across the years. This consensus, they contend, cuts across the Calvinist, Lutheran, Baptist, Arminian, Wesleyan, Holiness, charismatic, and Pentecostal streams of the evangelical church. Among these diverse evangelical denominations and theological movements, and despite the sometimes sharp and polemical attacks of their advocates on one another, there is a widely shared agreement about the central issues of Christian teaching.

This consensus includes foundational doctrines such as the authority of Holy Scriptures, belief in the one triune God, the creation and the fall, the personal work of Jesus Christ, justification by grace through faith, the sending of the Holy Spirit, the church as the sent-forth people of God, and the second coming of Christ.

A CALL FOR THEOLOGICAL RENEWAL . . . AND THE ROLE OF CREEDS

We believe that Packer and Oden are right. There is a discernable evangelical consensus, an agreement rooted in the historic orthodox faith of the church, reflecting the deepest biblical insights of the Reformation and shaped by the evangelistic and missionary impulses of the Great Awakening. Nonetheless, this consensus is more often assumed than articulated by evangelicals today. What the Presbyterian theologian John H. Leith wrote of his own mainline denomination regrettably applies to many evangelicals today: "The primary source of the malaise of the church is the loss of a distinctive Christian message and of the biblical and theological competence that made its preaching effective."[2]

Christian unity must be unity in the truth or it isn't worth having. This will require the evangelical church to pursue a holistic orthodoxy— a pursuit fueled by sustained theological renewal.

Theological renewal implies doctrinal boundaries, and, historically, such boundaries have been marked by churchly creeds, confessions, and statements of faith. It must be acknowledged, however, that for some evangelicals an explicitly confessional Christianity of this sort is problematic. "No Creed but the Bible" was a popular slogan of Alexander Campbell and the restorationist movement in the nineteenth century, but it expresses a view shared by many other non-creedal evangelicals as well.

We must acknowledge that there are some legitimate concerns raised by those who express reservations of this sort. The proper use of creeds and confessions is a good thing. Indeed, it is necessary for the kind of evangelical unity we are advocating. But evangelicals should avoid *creedalism* for several reasons. First, evangelicals do believe that God alone is Lord of the conscience. For this reason, among others, they are ardent supporters of religious liberty. Civil magistrates, while ordered by God for the proper maintenance of society, have no legitimate authority to coerce the conscience or to impose theological tests on the internal religious life of any church or community of faith. This is an important principle to remember in a world where religious freedom is still attacked in many places. To use creeds and other religious statements to enforce religious conformity is to confuse and misuse both the authority of the state and the teaching office of the church.

Further, evangelicals do not believe that any creed or humanly devised doctrinal construct should be elevated above Holy Scripture. The Bible alone remains the normative criterion for all teaching and instruction, "the supreme standard by which all human conduct, creeds, and religious opinions should be tried," as noted in one creedal statement ("The Baptist Faith and Message," I. Scripture). Because of this unswerving commitment to the priority and supremacy of Scripture, evangelicals have not "canonized" any of their confessions. This means that we hold all of our statements of faith to be revisable in light of the Bible, God's infallible, unchanging revelation.

With these qualifications in place, however, we believe that evangelical unity is enhanced by a proper use of creeds and confessions in our churches. The great Baptist, Charles Haddon Spurgeon, put it this way: "To the true believer a plain statement of his faith is no more a chain than a sword-belt to the soldier, or a girdle to the pilgrim."

STAYING ON THE ROAD:
STATEMENTS OF FAITH

How do such statements of faith serve the cause of evangelical unity? Perhaps they are best compared to the guardrails that help a driver, especially in bad weather, to negotiate the treacherously narrow roads and hairpin curves of a dangerous mountain highway. Such guardrails establish limits; they protect us from the dangers of the gaping ravines to our right and to our left. Only a fool with suicidal tendencies would want to drive across a range of mountains such as the Alps in Switzerland without guardrails. It would be equally foolish, of course, to mistake the guardrails for the road, for when we start driving on the rails it is certain that catastrophe is imminent!

For the Christian, there is only one road. Jesus said, "I am the way [road] and the truth and the life" (John 14:6). Or, as Augustine put it, Christ is "both our native country and himself also the road to that country." This analogy is not a perfect one, of course; still, we might push it a little further to say that the Bible is our road map, a divinely given and indispensable resource that helps us to find the road and keeps us on it, while the Holy Spirit helps us to see both the road and the guardrails and to keep them both in proper perspective.

DIFFERENCES MAJOR AND MINOR

We have argued that evangelical unity requires us to draw doctrinal boundaries in order to be faithful to Jesus Christ and to His Word. We have also said that there is an evangelical consensus that affirms the essence of biblical faith that can be garnered from evangelical statements of faith. These converging beliefs and teachings can unify, and they can form a sufficient basis for the kind of interdenominational, transcultural evangelistic and missionary enterprises in which evangelicals can— and have—worked together as a global Christian movement.

Such a view makes sense, however, only if we can distinguish those doctrines that are essential to the faith from others that, while certainly important, must be considered as secondary for the purposes of our common agreement in the unity of the gospel and our labors together in fulfilling the Great Commission of Jesus. The Puritan pastor Richard Baxter coined the phrase "mere Christianity," later made famous by C. S. Lewis, to describe the heart of what the New Testament calls "the faith once delivered to the saints." Baxter also gave currency to another statement that has been often quoted: "In things necessary, there must be unity; in things less than necessary, there must be liberty; and in all things, there must be charity." This is a wonderful statement and an ideal guideline for the kind of evangelical unity we would like to see more of in the life of the church today.

Baxter lived in an age when denominational lines were beginning to harden. He did not want to be called an Episcopalian, Presbyterian, or Congregationalist, he said, but rather a mere Christian. Baxter saw with clarity the connection between the desire for Christian unity and the evangelization of the lost. If Christians lived in the kind of love and unity Jesus called them to show forth, this would do wonders in converting sinners and enlarging the church of Jesus Christ. "Do not your hearts bleed to look upon the state of England," he asked, "and to think how few towns or cities there be (where is any forwardness in religion) that are not cut into shreds and crumbled as to dust by separations and divisions?"

When Baxter talked about "mere Christianity," he was not referring to "mere" in the weak, attenuated sense we so often do today. Both Baxter and Lewis used the word *mere* in what is today a regrettably obsolete sense, meaning "nothing less than," "absolute," "sure," "unqualified," as opposed to today's weakened sense of "only this," "nothing more than," "such and no more," "barely," "hardly."

Baxter had no use for a substanceless, colorless homogeneity bought at the expense of sound theology. He would have had no sympathy for the kind of "Doctrine Divides, Missions Unites" idea we have already encountered. No, for Baxter there were certain nonnegotiable fundamentals, including belief in one triune God; in one mediator between God and man, Jesus Christ, the eternal Word, God incarnate; and the Holy Spirit; and the gifts of God present to His covenanted people in baptism and holy communion; and in the life of obedience, holiness, and growth in Christ.

WHAT ARE THE ESSENTIALS?

What are the nonnegotiable essentials for evangelicals today? They include, at least, the Trinitarian and christological teachings of the early church and both the formal and material principles of the Reformation—that is, the normative authority of Holy Scripture and the doctrine of justification by grace alone, through faith alone, in Jesus Christ alone.

Who decides what is essential and what is secondary? Evangelicals will answer this question differently depending on their understanding of church governance—whether congregational, presbyterian, or episcopalian—but this is not as serious an impediment to evangelical unity as it might seem. While He was still on earth, Jesus promised to send the Holy Spirit to guide His disciples into deeper and further truth. The history of Christian doctrine reveals that Jesus has indeed fulfilled His promise. Despite heresies, deviations, and setbacks along the way, we can discern what might be called "the pattern of Christian truth," a theological trajectory that emerged in the struggles of the early church over the doctrine of God and the person of Christ, a consensus that received further clarification in the Reformation debates about sin, grace, and faith—a tradition to which evangelicals belong in their own efforts to read and interpret Scripture faithfully. In this sense, evangelicalism is best seen as a renewal movement within historic Christian orthodoxy.

This kind of perspective is necessary, we believe, if evangelicals are to distinguish the central affirmations of the faith from the peripheral, secondary issues that have become so divisive in our time. When the National Association of Evangelicals was founded in 1942, their motto was (and still is) "Cooperation Without Compromise." These neo-evangelicals, as they were soon called, were determined to stand together on the fundamentals of the faith and to cooperate with one another in ministry and witness to the wider culture without compromising either the historic Christian faith or their own denominational and biblical interpretive distinctions.

Thus, the evangelical coalition intentionally included both Calvinists and Arminians, both dispensationalists and covenantal theologians, both credobaptists and pedobaptists, both Pentecostals and non-charismatic believers. No one was asked to forego their biblical convictions about such matters, but there was an implicit call to work together in a unified front by properly distinguishing secondary and tertiary from primary matters of faith.

We think this paradigm is still a helpful one for evangelicals today, but it requires a serious theological vigilance. For example, in recent years one of the most hotly debated issues among evangelicals has been the so-called "openness of God" theology, a view that challenges the traditional Christian understanding that God has comprehensive knowledge of the future as well as of the present and the past. Some have argued that this issue should be regarded as a matter of tolerable diversity within the evangelical family, comparable to, say, the classic differences over predestination and free will or the role of women in ministry. Others have argued (we think convincingly) that this is a matter of different theological valence, for open theism proposes a revisionist understanding of God at odds not only with the evangelical consensus but also radically out of step with the historic Christian faith in all of its classic expressions—Roman Catholic, Orthodox, and Protestant alike. Our point here is not to enter into the details of that debate, but rather to stress the importance of ongoing theological rigor among evangelicals as we seek to maintain unity in love without compromising unity in truth.

SPEAKING THE TRUTH IN LOVE

At this point, let us summarize some of the things we have said thus far before moving forward to look once again at the counsel Francis Schaeffer gave to us in *The Mark of the Christian.* How can we maintain the unity of the Spirit in the bond of peace, speaking the truth to one another in love (Ephesians 4:3, 15), as the apostle Paul encouraged us to do? First, let's look at three paths we must not take in our quest for a harmonious result.

1. *We do not achieve unity by compromising our convictions.* Discussing matters about which Christians differed with one another, Paul said, "Each one should be fully convinced in his own mind. . . . Why do you judge your brother? Or why do you look down on your brother? For we will all stand before God's judgment seat" (Romans 14:5, 10).
2. *We must never seek togetherness for mere prudential reasons.* In the

same chapter in which Jesus prayed that His disciples might be one, He also asked the Father to sanctify them in the truth (John 17:17, 21). God's inerrant Word is the infallible standard to which we must always appeal in our efforts to understand the things of God more fully.

3. *We must never imagine that doctrinal matters are trivial or unimportant.* A church or theological institution with no doctrinal moorings, or one with shaky theological foundations, will soon have nothing to say to a lost and dying world. As we have seen, there is no such thing as missions apart from doctrine. Even those who claim to have no doctrines, or to be completely atheological, have simply bought into a different theology or ideology, namely, one that is shaped by indifference to truth.

Thinking constructively, how can we work together in a common Christian cause without violating these principles? Consider these suggestions:

First, make a careful distinction between primary doctrines of the faith, which may not be compromised without betraying the Gospel, *and secondary issues,* which may be important but are not essential for fellowship. Everything in God's Word is true and important or else it would not be there, but not everything is of equal importance in every respect. The second coming of Christ, for example, is a cardinal doctrine of the Christian faith. To deny it is to lapse into serious heresy. But earnest, Bible-believing Christians may honestly differ on some details of the end times without breaking fellowship with one another. Confessions of faith record the distinctive beliefs of local churches and various associations of Christians, and they can be very useful in helping Christians to distinguish primary and secondary matters of faith. But we must never forget that all such confessions are accountable to, and revisable in light of, the Bible.

Second, when we have theological disagreements with our brothers and sisters in Christ, it is always appropriate for us to pray for additional guidance and illumination from the Holy Spirit. John Robinson, the pastor of the Pilgrim fathers, once said to his flock: "The Lord has more truth and light yet to break forth out of His Holy Word." The same Spirit who inspired the Scriptures long ago must be present in our hearts and minds when we study them today if we are to understand them aright.

Third, humility, not arrogance, is the proper attitude in all controversies among Christians. This is not an argument for proceeding from lack of conviction, but rather for recognizing our own limitations and blind spots. The wisest among us are still learners in the school of faith.

SCHAEFFER AND "THE FINAL APOLOGETIC"

The Mark of the Christian was first published in 1970, near the end of Francis Schaeffer's long and distinguished career as a Christian thinker and apologist. Through his many writings and his engagement with the wider culture, Schaeffer taught an entire generation of younger Christian scholars—including the two of us—how to think Christianly in an emerging postmodern culture, one that even then was beginning to deny the very possibility of absolute truth. He appreciated intellectual rigor, and he knew the value of a sound argument.

Schaeffer also came from a sector of the evangelical community that greatly valued the importance of doctrinal truth. He belonged to a denomination that had itself split several times from other believers of similar persuasion over matters that were deemed at the time to be sufficiently important to warrant such drastic action.

In other words, Schaeffer was no easygoing ecumenist. He did not believe in blurring theological differences or papering over questions about baptism, church polity, or even eschatology in an effort to achieve an artificial harmony. He loved the truth, and he was irrevocably committed to theological integrity.

But near the end of his life, as he surveyed his own sometimes contentious ministry, and as he considered the increasingly fractious condition of evangelical church life in his day, he became convinced that Christians needed to recover what he called "the final apologetic," that is, the ability to love one another and to demonstrate that love in visible, observable ways before a watching world.

Schaeffer knew, of course, that Jesus commanded His disciples to love all persons made in the image of God, regardless of whether they were fellow believers or not. We have explored this Christian imperative of loving our neighbors in the previous chapter. But the New Testament also admonishes believers in Christ to give special attention to their relationships with their fellow Christians. For example, in Galatians 6:10 Paul wrote, "Therefore, as we have opportunity, let us do good to all people, especially to those who belong to the family of believers." A similar distinction can be discerned in 1 Thessalonians 3:12, "May the Lord make your love increase and overflow for each other and for everyone else, just as ours does for you."

THE MARK OF OUR IDENTITY:
SPECIAL BONDS OF AFFECTION

While not neglecting Jesus' command to love all of our neighbors as ourselves, Christians are exhorted to cherish and nurture the special bonds of affection that bind them to one another as brothers and sisters in the Lord. Why is this so important?

We can answer this question by asking another one: How were believers in Jesus recognized by the surrounding world in the early church? Clearly, they held certain distinctive beliefs, and they followed particular worship practices, such as baptism and the Lord's Supper. But to those on the outside, to pagans and unbelievers in general, such distinctives were hard to understand. For example, to many outside observers, the fact that Christians practiced a washing ritual called baptism and celebrated a community meal together sounded very much the pattern of worship in the various mystery religions of the Roman Empire. We hear an echo of such misunderstandings in the false charge of cannibalism leveled against the early Christians: Why were these strange people huddling together in dark corners to "eat the body and drink the blood" of someone?

Doctrine too could be misunderstood, as Paul found out when he preached about Jesus and the resurrection on Mars Hill in Athens. Many of the words Christians used—*logos* is a good example—were popular terms in Greek philosophy, and it took several generations, actually several centuries, for Christian theologians and apologists to distinguish in a clear, comprehensive way how these Greek terms had been given a radically new meaning by the reality of Jesus Christ.

So how are Christians to be recognized as Christians in such a world? Tertullian, a Christian writer living in Carthage at the end of the second century, gives us a glimpse of how unbelievers in that city saw the Christians of his day:

> We are a body knit together as such by a common religious profession, by unity of discipline, and by the bond of a common hope. We meet together as an assembly and congregation, that, offering up prayer to God as with united force, we may wrestle with him in our supplications. . . . [Our gifts] are not spent on feasts, and drinking-bouts, and eating-houses, but to support and bury poor people, to supply the wants of boys and girls destitute of means and parents, and of old persons confined now to the house; such, too, as have suffered shipwreck; and if there happens to be any in the mines, or banished to the islands, or shut up in the prisons, for nothing but their fidelity to the cause of God's church, they become the nurslings of their confession. But it is mainly the deeds of a love so noble that lead many to put a brand upon us. *See,* they say, *how they love one another!*[3]

Christians were known in Carthage, even by their enemies, as a group of people who were motivated and marked by their great love for one another.

In holding forth love as the distinguishing mark of the church, Jesus made two statements with awesome implications, as Francis Schaeffer pointed out in his classic study. First, Jesus gave the world the right to decide whether we are really Christians based upon our observable love for one another. "By this all men will know that you are my disciples, if you love one another" (John 13:35). Jesus was not saying here that we will lose our salvation if we act in an unloving way toward one another. But He was saying that unbelievers in the world will likely conclude, and that they have a right to conclude, that we really don't know Jesus at all if we live in bitterness, contention, and rancor with one another. They may well be wrong in the conclusion they draw (that we are not true Christians), but we will have contributed to their own hardening and walking away from the Gospel because of our unloving acts and attitudes toward one another.

Remember, people are not able to peer into our hearts. Unbelievers cannot know the true status of our relationship with God. But they can hear our words and see our lives. And on the basis of what they observe, Jesus said, they have a right to draw a conclusion about the genuineness of our faith in Christ.

Second, Jesus asked in His prayer on Gethsemane, "That all of them may be one, Father, just as you are in me and I am in you. May they also be in us so that the world may believe that you have sent me" (John 17:21). In John 13, Jesus gave the world the right to judge whether anyone is a true Christian based upon how that person treats his or her fellow believers in Christ. Now Jesus says something even more sobering. As Schaeffer put it, "We cannot expect the world to believe that the Father sent the Son, that Jesus' claims are true, that Christianity is true, unless the world sees some reality of the oneness of true Christians."

This is our final apologetic before the world—observable oneness in Christ manifested by a visible love that goes beyond pious platitudes to include mutual forgiveness, humility, and a willingness to forego our own prerogatives in order to build up the body of Christ.

THE TRUE TEST OF LOVE:
WHEN WE DISAGREE

It is easy to pay lip service to love. Who is against love? The problem is that we trivialize love by not practicing it, or by pretending that we can practice love without it costing us anything. The true test here is how Christians relate to one another in times of disagreement. In the midst of church splits or denominational divisions, how often have we heard public declarations of love followed almost immediately by statements of recrimination and character assassination? Even if the concern that led to such a division is right and godly, such as upholding the truth of Scripture or maintaining the purity of the church, when harsh,

uncharitable comments are spread throughout the community, or publicly plastered in the press, scars are created that can last for generations. Incalculable harm is often done to the cause of Christ.

Schaeffer used the strong word *stench* to describe the ill effects of such
Christian ugliness:

> I have observed one thing among *true Christians* in their differences in
> many countries: what divides and severs true Christian groups and Chris-
> tians—what leaves a bitterness that can last for twenty, thirty, or forty
> years (or fifty or sixty years in a son's memory)—is not the issue of doc-
> trinal belief which caused the differences in the first place. Invariably it is
> lack of love—and the bitter things that are said by true Christians in the
> midst of differences. These stick in the mind like glue. And after time
> passes and the differences between the Christians or the groups appear
> less than they did, there are still those bitter, bitter things we said in the
> midst of what we thought was a good and objective discussion. It is these
> things—these unloving attitudes and words—that cause the stench that
> the world can smell in the church of Jesus Christ among those who are
> really true Christians.[4]

COSTLY LOVE FOR
OUR FELLOW BELIEVERS

The mark of Jesus is love, costly love, and it does not come naturally
or easily. It requires us to be willing to say sincerely some of the most difficult words we can speak: "I'm sorry"; "Will you forgive me?"; "I may
have been wrong"; "Can we pray together about this?"; "Can we still
work together, in some things if not in everything?"; "I love you." Such
words must be followed by deeds, costly deeds, that demonstrate nothing less than the highest standard possible or imaginable. It is the standard of Jesus' own love for us.

We are to love all Christians, Jesus said, "as I have loved you." No,
we cannot do this perfectly. Jesus was the Son of God, sinless in every
way. We are sinners who have been rescued by divine grace, and we are
still prone to backsliding, mistakes, and failures every day. But we can-

not use this fact as an excuse to evade Jesus' command. We are to love one another *as He has loved us.* Nothing less will do. We are to demonstrate His quality of love; His commitment to serve rather than to be served; His undying compassion for the least, the last, and the lost; His willingness to go all the way to the cross, saying over and over again as He died, "Father forgive, forgive, forgive, forgive."

This, and nothing less, is the standard of love we are to demonstrate to one another. This is the mark of Jesus the world is still waiting to see.

When the World
Calls Us Hypocrites
How Should
We Respond?

Have you ever thought that Christians sometimes fail to get a fair shake from critics in the culture at large? You are not an alarmist, nor are you resistant to deserved criticism for errors or wrongdoing. Rather, you have in mind specific incidents in which critics did not fairly present the beliefs and actions of Christians.

When two Christian leaders criticized the founder of Islam, syndicated columnist Molly Ivins wrote a searing rejoinder in which she accused Christians in general of hypocrisy: "Let's see, where does that leave Christianity, the religion of peace and love, founded by the Prince of Peace? Among the more notable Christian crimes were the unbearably bloody Crusades, the Thirty Years War, the Inquisition, innumerable pogroms, regular slaughter of Protestants, counter slaughter by Protestants, genocide against Native Americans . . . , slavery, the Holocaust, ethnic cleansing, Northern Ireland . . . and the list goes on and on and on. People who live in glass houses shouldn't throw stones."[1] From Ivins' perspective, Christians are "hypocritical," and thus disqualified from making any moral judgments about others.

Similarly, after the 2004 presidential election, some political commentators claimed, according to another syndicated columnist, that "vengeful Christian zealots" (i.e., evangelicals) had embarked on "a hatchet-wielding jihad against heathens, pagans and infidels."[2]

Keeping in mind we are to bear the mark of Jesus in loving our neighbors as ourselves, how should we respond when encountering criticisms of this kind? More specifically, how should we interact with critics' charges in a way that honors the Lord?

Responding in a Christlike fashion is no easy matter. This is especially the case if we rely solely on our own strength. We find it very difficult to think well of those who criticize us. If we are angry, we may want to hit back. If we feel hurt, we may nurse grudges against our critics, sometimes for years. Not only can powerful feelings of hurt and revenge rob us of our sense of joy and peace in the Lord; they hinder us from reaching out to these same people with generosity and love. One reason John Wesley was thought to have had success in ministry was that he tried to forget slights.

How should we conduct ourselves when faced with criticism, especially the charge that we are hypocrites? In this discussion we will first consider the various ways critics have packaged the hypocrisy charge against Christians, for the charge comes in different wrappings. Second, we will consider biblical teaching about hypocrisy, especially Christ's strong warnings against it. Third, we will consider the way Christians of the early church faced hypocrisy charges as compared with the way evangelicals are dealing with the charges today. Finally, we will consider ways we can respond ourselves should we face hypocrisy charges.

THE NEWS MEDIA AND HYPOCRISY CHARGES

Ivins and other critics in the news media who charge Christians with hypocrisy often have had relatively little contact with them, especially evangelical believers. Columnist Nicholas D. Kristof admits as much:

"Claims that the news media form a vast liberal conspiracy strike me as utterly unconvincing, but there's one area where accusations of institutional bias have merit: nearly all of us in the news business are completely out of touch with a group that includes 46 percent of Americans. That's the proportion who described themselves in a Gallup poll in December as evangelical or born again Christians."[3]

Members of the media often have little understanding of what ordinary Americans think. An editor for the *Chicago Tribune* acknowledged how difficult it is for members of the media to grasp the beliefs of persons who are not "liberal" and "pro-gay" in one editorial: "We have trouble *seeing reality* from the perspectives of those who do not fit into the newsroom 'mainstream,' which, according to recent surveys for the Project for Excellence in Journalism and the Committee of Concerned Journalists, is predominantly 'liberal' and 'moderate' and overwhelmingly convinced that homosexuality should be accepted by society."[4]

The media are not totally to blame for their inability to understand the thought of "those persons who are not 'liberal' and 'pro-gay.'" Often we, as evangelical Christians, have shied away from participating in the media and the arts. With few Christian dialogue partners to propose other ways of looking at the world, it is not surprising that "liberal elites" of the media often assume their views on abortion, radical feminism, pornography, and the law are simply the ways "good," informed people should think about them.

Some "liberal elites" really do perceive the world in an upside-down fashion from the way many ordinary, conservative Americans do. In *Arrogance: Rescuing America from the Media Elite* (Warner, 2003), Bernard Goldberg writes: "No matter how they cast it or try to dodge the issue, to most in the big-time media, a liberal is, by definition, a good guy, someone who is decent and compassionate. A conservative, on the other hand, by definition is a selfish, mean-spirited moral slug."

The media's lack of firsthand contacts with evangelical Christians has not hindered a number of their well-known representatives from flaying Christians as hypocrites. All it takes to provoke these critics is for Christians to affirm that Jesus Christ is *the* way, *the* truth, and *the* life (John 14:6). This claim allegedly provides irrefutable proof that Christians, who profess love and concern for others, are lying and thus incorrigible hypocrites. After all, no person who truly loves someone else and is genuinely tolerant could conceivably believe that people are "spiritually lost" apart from Christ. Christians' claims that they believe in civil rights and religious tolerance can be dismissed for what they are—hypocritical, empty rhetoric.

Newspaper columnists and television and radio newscasters engage in some of the most effective criticism of conservative Christians when they indiscriminately use the word *fundamentalist* to describe Mideastern terrorists (more on the "fundamentalist" tag in the next chapter). In doing this, they link, at least by indirect connotation, those American Christians who call themselves fundamentalists with terrorists. This is a most unfair ideological coupling. Not for a moment have the overwhelming majority of these Christians entertained the thought they should resort to violence or terrorist activity. Unfortunately, critics dismiss as laughable hypocrisy any claims by fundamentalists that they believe in the power of Christian love and are concerned about the social needs of their neighbors.

Goldberg points out that the liberal media often neglect stories about the "good things" people do, including the many good things Christians do. By contrast, when a well-known pastor or evangelist falls into sin, many reporters rush to ferret out the unsavory details. Reporting on a pastor's sins and hypocrisy makes for sensational newspaper copy and can garner bold headlines. Certainly sins should not be covered up. It appears, however, that members of the media often receive particular delight in disclosing sins committed by "religious" people. If "religious people" commit the same sins as everyone else, then these sins are probably not so bad after all. Moreover, why should any non-Christian heed the moral admonitions or the Gospel message if Christians are by and large hypocrites?

THE ENTERTAINMENT MEDIA
AND HYPOCRISY CHARGES

The theme of the hypocritical Christian pervades motion pictures, theater, and television. In *Hollywood vs. America: Popular Culture and the*

War on Traditional Values (Perennial, 1993), Michael Medved chronicled in sobering detail Hollywood's no-quarter-given assault on "traditional values" in the early 1990s. The attack has not let up. Moviemakers, for example, continue to relish portraying Christians as hypocrites. Believers often appear as unfaithful in marriages, seducers, racists, and intellectual dolts. By contrast, movie directors present characters who attempt to remove the vestiges of Christian morality as attractively edgy, freedom loving, and daring rule breakers. For example, a film like *XXX* glorifies a character who helps save the planet while at the same time habitually breaking all the rules.

The hypocrisy of Christians resides as the central motif of a number of musicals. The acclaimed musical opera *Susannah* (1955, with many reprises, including 2002) tells the story of a young woman who is seduced by Reverend Olin Blitch, a "Bible thumping itinerant preacher." In a review of this opera, John von Rhein, a *Chicago Tribune* music critic, painted New Hope Valley, a town apparently populated with a good number of Christians and the fictional site of the story in the Appalachians, in the most unflattering manner: ". . . a remote community where prejudice, jealousy and moral superiority lurk just below the puritanical surface."

EDUCATION AND HYPOCRISY CHARGES

In the field of education, critics often wrap the hypocrisy charge against Christians in subtler but no less effective ways. For example, should Christian students speak favorably about the values and beliefs of the Puritans, a "politically correct" teacher may condescendingly suggest that the students are narrow-minded and ethical absolutists. If Christian parents should propose in a school board meeting that other views of origins besides naturalistic evolution deserve a hearing in public schools, well-respected educators may dismiss them as religious fanatics who are hypocritically trying to foist off their religion under the guise of "science." If Christian parents should complain about an obvious pro-homosexual agenda pushed by certain faculty members at a high school, school administrators may castigate the parents as attempting to impose their religious values upon others, and as intolerant bigots who are "homophobic."

Critics who are "ethical relativists" commonly contend that religion is a totally private matter; it should not influence public education or public policy in any prescriptive manner. Stanford Professor Richard Rorty explains: "The main reason religion needs to be privatized is that, in political discussion with those outside the relevant community, it is a conversation stopper."

Such charges and arguments may catch Christian believers off guard. Are statements of belief by Christians not guaranteed by the First Amendment, which proclaims freedom of speech regarding religion? Do not the guidelines of the U.S. Department of Education (1998, 2003) read: "Students may express their beliefs about religion on homework, artwork, and other written and oral assignments free from discrimination based on the religious content of their submissions"? Is it not true that the nation's founding fathers had no intention of separating church from state in such a way as to forbid religious expression in the public square?

Yet despite the critics' accusations, upholding the exclusivist claim about Christ renders Christians automatically hypocritical, insincere, unloving, and incapable of endorsing the rights of conscience for people of other religious persuasions. Further, Christians can object to the promotion of a homosexual lifestyle in a public school while simultaneously still showing Christian love and respect toward homosexuals.

THE CHALLENGE FOR CHRISTIAN PARENTS

The parents of grade school children often feel especially concerned about "hypocrisy" charges. They wonder what negative influence these accusations will exercise upon their children's perceptions of the Christian faith. If a child comes home and indicates that her teacher taught that the Pilgrims and Puritans founded the New England colonies primarily for economic gain, that they pillaged the lands and goods of the Indians and promoted "sexual repression," what should the parents say?

Relatively few Christian parents are professional historians. Yet many know such an interpretation is grossly one-sided and stands in need of serious revision. Puritans like John Winthrop and John Cotton came to the New World essentially for religious reasons, not principally as participants in a vanguard for mercantilism ("economic nationalism"). In his *Magnalia Christi Americana,* Cotton Mather, while acknowledging the role of "economic" motivations for the settlements, indicated that the major reasons the early Puritans ventured to New England were to escape religious persecution and to bring the Gospel to the Indians. In an oft-quoted statement, John Winthrop also asserted that the Puritans should be a "city upon a hill" from which the light of the Christian faith would shine.

What's more, some parents may know that Perry Miller, the pre-eminent Puritan historian of the twentieth century, though an atheist, did not dismiss the Puritans as intellectual dullards. Rather, he praised their mental acumen and the "machinery" of their theological beliefs. In writing about "the perplexing Puritans," Miller overthrew the long-standing caricature of the Puritans as killjoys who were always dressed in black and had a black steeple hat perched on their heads. Rather, the Puritans wore clothing that sported all the "hues of the rainbow." Nor were the Puritans sexually repressed prudes who did not enjoy the beauty of God's creation.

How Parents Can Respond to Biased Teaching

Aware of these clarifications, should parents take the initiative to speak graciously with their children's teachers? Undoubtedly, some teachers might resent suggestions that other interpretations of the Puritans than their own are persuasive. At the same time, certain teachers will welcome specific references to reputable books regarding another perspective on the Puritans. One such book is Leland Ryken's *Worldly Saints: The Puritans as They Really Were* (Zondervan, 1986). In the foreword to the book, J. I. Packer writes: "The sport of slinging mud has had a wide following. Pillorying the Puritans, in particular, has long been a popular pastime on both sides of the Atlantic." For his part, Ryken indicates that one of the major purposes of his book is "to correct an almost universal misunderstanding of what the Puritans really stood for."

Relatively few Christian parents are professional scientists. Nonetheless, they know that the case for naturalistic evolution is far from "proven." Materialism cannot explain satisfactorily the irreducible complexity of even simple living organisms. Design arguments for God's existence have gained new credence in the larger academic world, not just in the ranks of evangelical scholars. Nonetheless, some public school educators, unaware of new scholarship, continue to teach as if materialism is the only intellectually respectable worldview educated persons may entertain. The textbooks these teachers choose will often assume a materialist explanation of origins.

As a parent, should you question the instruction of your children's teachers who promote atheistic naturalism as the only basis for science? Will the educators dismiss an appeal for an equitable presentation of various views on origins as rank hypocrisy and as a cloak for religious prejudice?

Once again, some teachers might do just that. Others, however, might appreciate learning about a book like Phillip Johnson's *Darwin on Trial.* Johnson, who taught law at the University of California (Berkeley), raises serious objections concerning the legitimacy of naturalistic evolution.

For Christian parents, bearing the mark of Jesus when faced by public school teachers militantly committed to discrediting Christian values is no easy matter. But even in this circumstance, the Holy Spirit can give grace and wisdom. Moreover, many public school teachers, whether Christian or not, do present materials in an equitable manner.

Educators Who Discredit Christian Values

Other educators, both public school teachers and college-level professors—often under the guise of separating out religion from the public sphere—are ideologically driven. In pursuing their mission, they may rely on the "hypocrisy" trump card to drive home their points.

Some public educators argue, "Christians say they are interested in the objective study of science, but they are in fact hypocrites, trying to import their religious beliefs into state educational curricula."

On the public university level, many professors advocate an atheistic naturalism, causing historian George Marsden to conclude that "in effect, the only points of view that are allowed full academic credence are those that presuppose purely naturalistic worldviews."[5] In the universities, critics of Christianity resort to the "hypocrisy charge" on a regular basis. The charge becomes especially persuasive when wrapped in "everyone knows" truisms. The "everyones" are allegedly all "educated persons."

For example, in certain "women's studies programs," "everyone knows" that those Christians who oppose lesbianism are repressive, intolerant people. In certain religious studies programs, "everyone knows" that Western Christians were warmongering imperialists; they launched crusades against Muslims; they fought ruthlessly among themselves in a whole series of religious wars; and Christian missionaries in the nineteenth century plied native peoples with the Gospel in preparation for "Christian" businessmen to sell them European and American products. In certain American studies programs, "everyone knows" that Christians inculcated views of sexual repression into the thinking of colonial America that only the "sexual revolution" of the 1960s could begin to heal.

With these "truisms" so prevalent on campus and so rarely challenged, little wonder that many students conclude Christianity is a "repressive" religion.

RESPONDING TO THE HYPOCRISY CHARGE

How should we respond as Christians to the "hypocrisy charge," whatever its packaging? One response would be for us to do nothing. We can simply ignore any criticisms of the beliefs and lifestyles of Christians past and present. A second response might be to assume a strongly defensive posture. We can try to parry all criticisms, attempting to prove they are false accusations. A third response might be to recognize, when appropriate, the validity of particular charges and to call for sincere confession and restitution.

Each of these responses can create a dilemma for us. If we choose the no-response first option, we may very well let untruths stand. If we become hypersensitive to criticism, we might pursue the second option and end up defending Christians against charges that are in fact valid. If we choose the third response, and fail to speak carefully and humbly, we may engage in a large-scale indictment of our brothers and sisters in Christ that is not only unfair but reveals the existence of an arrogant spirit within us.

Paradoxically enough, if we decide to respond to critics at all, we can become "hypocritical" even in the way we argue that we are not "hypocritical." We can state our cases brilliantly while showing little concern for the welfare of our opponent. We can be more desirous that our audiences admire our debating skills than be genuinely concerned that they come to a better understanding of the Christian faith.

Dealing with the hypocrisy charge in a way that pleases the Lord demands Christian humility, wisdom, and love. If we are not empowered by the Holy Spirit, we will find it very difficult to bear the mark of Jesus while attempting to answer this charge.

What the General Public Sees

Even if we have not reflected very much about how serious the hypocrisy charge is, many non-Christians in the culture at large have obviously done so. Non-Christians are often very discerning observers of how well Christians' words and actions mesh with their beliefs. Respect for religious institutions among Christians and non-Christians alike generally tumbles after church leaders are perceived as hypocritical.

According to a Gallup Poll, from 1973 to the mid-1980s more than 60 percent of Americans held a favorable attitude toward religious institutions. Then in the late 1980s, the televangelist scandals broke (involving Jim Bakker, Jimmy Swaggart, and others) for all to see. Americans' confidence level in religious institutions fell rapidly to 52 percent. At the beginning of the new millennium (toward 2001), the confidence level had climbed back up to 59 percent only to fall again precipitously to 45 percent in 2002 after revelations dominated the media about abuses perpetrated by members of the Roman Catholic Church clergy.

No wonder Molly Ivins castigated the clergy in one column, calling them "pietistic hypocrites and spiritual humbugs wearing dog collars." Comments like this one help us understand the seriousness of the hypocrisy charge, even if wrapped in a false accusation. For many, the perception that the charge is in fact true can create genuine barriers for a fair hearing of the Gospel.

Biblical Warnings: When Two Faces Are One Too Many

As Christians, we need to take the charge of hypocrisy very seriously. Christ certainly did. Jesus declared, "Why do you look at the speck of sawdust in your brother's eye and pay no attention to the plank in your own eye? How can you say to your brother, 'Let me take the speck out of your eye,' when all the time there is a plank in your own eye? You hypocrite, first take the plank out of your own eye, and then you will see clearly to remove the speck from your brother's eye" (Matthew 7:3–5).

When we criticize another Christian, we sometimes experience a rush of feelings of self-righteous superiority (spiritual pride) toward the other person, even though we may be secretly harboring sins ourselves. Jonathan Edwards shrewdly observed that this kind of spiritual pride is a principal culprit in clogging the work of the Holy Spirit in a person's ministry. By contrast, genuine humility sets a person further aside from the Evil One's reach and makes a person more available for service for the Lord.

When we parade our spirituality before others in long prayers, heartrending testimonies, and polished preaching and at the same time harbor unconfessed sin, we are nakedly two-faced. Jesus Christ condemned all such hypocritical posturing: "Woe to you, teachers of the law and Pharisees, you hypocrites! You are like whitewashed tombs, which look beautiful on the outside but on the inside are full of dead men's bones and everything unclean. In the same way, on the outside you appear to people as righteous but on the inside you are full of hypocrisy and wickedness" (Matthew 23:27–28).

To escape hypocrisy's subtle allures, it is very important for us to grow in grace by seeking after Christ. Commenting on 2 Peter 3:18,

Charles Spurgeon wrote: "He who does not long to know more of Christ, knows nothing of Him yet. . . . An increase of love to Jesus, and a more perfect apprehension of His love for us is one of the best tests of growth in grace."[6]

Empowered by the Holy Spirit, we should seek to do everything with a clear conscience. For us to enjoy a good conscience, we must keep short accounts with God by regularly confessing our sins (1 John 1:9). We should daily bear the mark of the Christian in loving God and our neighbor. Paul wrote: "The goal of this command is love, which comes from a pure heart and a good conscience and a sincere faith" (1 Timothy 1:5). Elsewhere Paul tells us to abstain from sin: "'Everyone who confesses the name of the Lord must turn away from wickedness'" (2 Timothy 2:19). With the Holy Spirit's help we should do everything possible to refrain from sin that throws disrepute on the cause of Christ, weighs us down personally with a "bad conscience," and converts us into hypocrites.

Hypocrisy is a form of play-acting in which we profess a Christian conviction and then violate it. Hypocrisy can be habit-forming—a genuine addiction. We get used to being two-faced. We wear a mask and pretend to be something or someone we are not. We forget that we are forgiven sinners saved by grace. We are afraid to drop our mask and let people know what we are really like. *Will they still think highly of me if they really know what sometimes goes through my mind and the things I sometimes do?*

Hypocrisy subverts our Christian walk. We shrivel up spiritually inside. We worry whether or not we will be found out. In late nineteenth-century Britain, a prankster apparently sent messages at random to a number of religious leaders. Each message bore the same warning: "You have been discovered. All will be revealed." The prankster did not, in fact, have sordid information about any of the recipients of the messages. He just supposed religious leaders were often hypocrites.

Suddenly, more than half the persons who had received the messages resigned their clerical posts—this to the total surprise of their congregations. The prankster believed he knew why the religious leaders had taken this precipitous step: They feared that what they had done in private would be disclosed publicly.

When we are hypocritical, we lose our desire to tell other people about Christ. We find it difficult to get the words out of our mouth about how becoming a Christian gives a person spiritual power and joy or the abundant life when we ourselves have not recently experienced this spiritual power and joy we say comes with following Christ.

Hypocrisy destroys our fellowship with our heavenly Father and with other believers. The apostle John wrote: "If we claim to have fellowship with him yet walk in the darkness, we lie and do not live by the truth. But if we walk in the light, as he is in the light, we have fellowship with one another, and the blood of Jesus, his Son, purifies us from all sin" (1 John 1:6–7). Hypocrisy and lying are twins, or at least siblings.

Finally, the hypocrisy of Christians provides unbelievers with a remarkable excuse to not consider the Gospel. After all, why should they listen to a message from people who testify to its transformative power but are obviously hypocrites? Many non-Christians feel fully justified in repeating these familiar refrains:

"Christians do not practice what they preach."

"Christians profess what they don't possess."

"Go to church? Are you kidding? Churches are full of hypocrites. I know because I used to go to church."

Philosopher Jean-Paul Sartre, whose conversion is addressed in the introduction, delayed his decision until the end of his life in part because of the hypocrisy charge. When an evangelical Christian witnessed to him, Sartre responded: "I understand what you are saying, but you know, there are so many so-called Christians. . . . When I see the actions of certain persons like that, I am not able to believe."

THE HYPOCRISY CHARGE AND
THE EARLY CHURCH (A.D. 33–500)

In the 1670s, a Lutheran pastor in northern Germany became very concerned about the worldliness of his contemporaries. Jacob Spener believed that many church members professed orthodox belief but lived manifestly unchristian lives. They were in fact flagrant hypocrites. These people cited their belief in justification by faith alone as a doctrine that legitimized or at least explained their continued sinning.

In *Pious Desires* (*Pia Desideria*, 1675), Spener argued that a better spiritual state for Christians must be possible. Why? Because Scripture promised such: "If we consult the Holy Scriptures, we can have no doubt that God promised his church here on earth a better state than this." Then Spener went on to point out that the early Christians gave an authentic example of how people can be Christ's disciples: "The condition of the early Christian church puts our hot-and-cold condition to shame. At the same time it demonstrates that what we are seeking is not impossible as many imagine." Providing even further hope for better days, Spener reminded his readers that the same Holy Spirit who spiritually empowered the early Christians was available to Christians of their own day. Consequently, reform and renewal of the Christian churches were indeed possible.

Certainly, hypocrites and heretics existed in the early church. But the early Christians, recognizing how serious heresy and hypocrisy were, tried to deal with both problems directly. They drafted creeds and "rules of faith" in which they defined what orthodox belief was. Moreover, they practiced sturdy church discipline.

Nero's Cruel Charge

Just like Christians of our day, believers in the early church had to confront the accusation that they were hypocrites. Critics often served up this accusation, and that in turn stirred up persecution against believers.

In the *Annales* (15, 44), Tacitus, a noted Roman historian, reported that when Rome was set ablaze in A.D. 64, the Roman emperor Nero accused the Christians of the city of setting the fire. Tacitus surmised that Nero made this false accusation to cover up his own role in having ordered the fire set: "But all the endeavors of men, all the emperor's largesse and the propitiations of the gods, did not suffice to allay the scandal or banish the belief that the fire had been ordered. And so, to get rid of this rumor, Nero set up as the culprits and punished with the utmost refinement of cruelty a class hated for their abominations, who are commonly called Christians." As Tacitus explained, many Christians experienced horrible deaths: "Besides being put to death they were made to serve as objects of amusement; they were clad in the hides of beasts and torn to death by dogs; others were crucified, others set on fire to serve to illuminate the night when daylight failed."

Haters of the Human Race?

Although Tacitus felt tinges of sympathy for the plight of the suffering Christians, he concurred that they deserved death. He claimed in particular that the Christians evidenced a heinous attitude, that is, "hatred of the human race."

What a galling false accusation for Roman Christians to endure. They had in all likelihood declared their intention to love the true God with all their hearts, soul, and minds and their neighbors as themselves, and then they were hit with this charge. The accusation had a devastating implication: Christians, in affirming that they loved their fellow Romans, were hypocrites of the first order.

Many Romans did believe that Christians were "haters of the human race." To them, the Christians' refusal to participate in the rites and games associated with the worship of the Roman gods and the practice of good citizenship appeared sufficient grounds to make the charge stick.

Other Charges . . . and Martyrdom

According to Athengoras, the early Christians faced a number of other false charges: "Three things are alleged against us: atheism, Thyestean feasts, Oedipodean intercourse." The Romans deemed Christians arrogant atheists: They did not believe in the Roman gods. The Romans deemed Christians cannibalistic: They spoke of eating of their Savior's body (during the Lord's Supper). The Romans deemed Christians incestuous (oedipodean): They spoke about loving their brothers and sisters. The Romans even deemed Christians baby killers (infanticide). The Romans also depicted Christians as seditious members of secret societies.

The Romans' misunderstanding of the Christians' lifestyles and worship practices was often profound. Romans sometimes felt what they thought was righteous indignation towards the Christians. They could believe themselves fully justified in persecuting these morally perverse and seditious renegades.

In *The Christians as the Romans Saw Them* (1984), historian Robert Wilken wrote that the Romans regarded Christians "as religious fanatics, self-righteous outsiders, arrogant innovators, who thought that only their beliefs were true."

Paul's teaching in Romans 8 undoubtedly provided much-needed solace to the Roman Christians who faced martyrdom during Nero's horrific persecution of A.D. 64. Paul had written comforting words to the church of the very people Nero was going to transform into pitiful, human torches: "Who shall separate us from the love of Christ?" he asked, noting the "trouble or hardship or persecution . . . or danger or sword" that visited some. The truth, Paul wrote, is that "in all these things we are more than conquerors through him who loved us. For I am convinced that neither death nor life, neither angels nor demons, neither the present nor the future, nor any powers, neither height nor depth, nor anything else in all creation, will be able to separate us from the love of God that is in Christ Jesus our Lord" (Romans 8:35, 37–39).

According to tradition, Paul was martyred in A.D. 64. In his *Ecclesiastical History,* Eusebius wrote, "Thus Nero publicly announcing himself as the chief enemy of God, was led on in his fury to slaughter the apostles. Paul is therefore said to have been beheaded at Rome, and Peter to have been crucified under him."

The way the early church lived and died remains a model of what Christianity is like when the faith is authentically embraced. During Nero's persecution, Roman Christians apparently had little chance to respond to the false accusations, including any that purported they were hypocrites. Believers were quite summarily put to death.

By the second century, however, the Romans had developed the rudiments of a legal procedure for putting Christians on trial. The correspondence between Pliny the Younger and the Emperor Trajan reveals its emerging guidelines. Christians had an opportunity to escape death if they would deny Christ and demonstrate this by worshiping the "genius" (spirit) of Caesar. They were urged to curse Christ.

The Testimony of Justin Martyr

Justin Martyr effectively depicted and defended the lifestyle of Christians. In his *First Apology* (c. A.D. 155), Justin challenged Emperor Antonius Pius to take a good, hard look at the way Christians lived. Justin apparently did not fear that an investigation by the emperor would find the Christians to be hypocrites: "It is for us, therefore, to offer to all the opportunity of inspecting our life and teachings, lest we ourselves should bear the blame for what those who do not really know about us do in their ignorance."

Then, in a marvelous passage, Justin described how the power of the Gospel had transformed Christians at the very core of their aspirations and desires:

> Those who once rejoiced in fornication now delight in continence alone; those who made use of magic arts have dedicated themselves to the good and unbegotten God; we who once took pleasure in the means of increasing our wealth and property now bring what we have into a common fund and share with everyone in need; we who hated and killed one another would not associate with men of different tribes because of [their different] customs, now after the manifestation of Christ live together and pray for our enemies and try to persuade those who unjustly hate us, so that they, living according to the fair command of Christ may share with us the good hope of receiving the same things [that we will] from God, the master of all.[7]

According to Martyr, Christians turned their backs on sexual immorality, on the making of money as a life avocation, and on yielding to racism. Rather, they shared their goods even with those whom they had formerly disdained for racial reasons—those who belonged to other tribes. Many Christians were living in unity and were intent on seeing their non-Christian neighbors come to Christ. They prayed for their enemies with the hope that they might likewise become followers of the true God. They believed that only those persons were worthy to be called Christians who actually obeyed their Lord's teachings.

As for those persons who did not obey Christ's teachings (hypocrites), Justin Martyr offered little comfort: "Those who are found not living as he taught should know that they are not really Christians, even if his teachings are on their lips, for he said that not those who merely profess but those who also do the works will be saved. For he said this: 'Not everyone who says to me, Lord, Lord, will enter into the Kingdom of Heaven, but he who does the will of my Father who is in heaven.'"

Justin Martyr, therefore, viewed "apologetics" (the defense of the faith) in a somewhat different fashion than we often do, if we limit its scope to the presentation of the "theistic proofs" or historical arguments for the resurrection of Christ. Certainly Martyr made the case for fulfilled prophecies in Scripture, the reality of Christ's miracles, and the truthfulness of the resurrection. But Martyr was not hesitant also to make the point that many of the Christians he knew obeyed Christ's teachings. This would mean that any hypocrisy charge regarding them would not stick. He wrote: "Many men and women now in their sixties and seventies who have been disciples of Christ from childhood have preserved their purity: and I am proud that I could point to such people in every nation."

Justin Martyr's presentation of how Christians actually lived out their faith received confirmation of sorts from a surprising quarter. Pagan critics, while condemning Christianity as an irrational faith that attracted the weak-minded, on occasion paid backhanded tributes to the Christians by describing them as those who kept their word and shared their goods with each other.

Undoubtedly, the early church had its hypocrites who by no means followed Christ in the way Justin Martyr indicated. At the end of the second century, Tertullian complained that he knew Christians, including members of the clergy, who ran after money and church offices rather than seeking to follow Christ's teachings. For many early Christians, not following Christ's teachings indicated a person was worse than a hypocrite; the person was a "non-Christian."

Eusebius labeled as "impostors" those who hypocritically professed

Christianity but did not practice the faith. Christians could be fooled by these heretical "impostors" and "deceivers" who could also give true Christianity a bad reputation by their acts and beliefs. He argued in *The Ecclesiastical History* (book 4, chapter 7) that as the Christian faith continued to spread, the Evil One turned to new strategies to attack the church:

> He [the Evil One] then waged a war by other methods, in which he employed the agency of wicked impostors as certain abandoned instruments and minions of destruction. Intent upon every course, he instigated these insidious impostors and deceivers, by assuming the same name with us (Christians) to lead those believers whom they happened to seduce to the depths of destruction and by their presumption, also turned those that were ignorant of the faith, from the path that led to the saving truth of God.

Christians, then, found themselves facing a war on multiple fronts: "imposters" and "deceivers" (hypocrites and heretics) within the camp and pagan critics outside.

More Accusations after the Edict of Milan (A.D. 313)

Along with the co-emperor Licinius, Constantine granted much welcomed toleration for Christians in the Edict of Milan (A.D. 313). Nonetheless, during the next century, Christians continued to confront critics who drew up fresh complaints against them. For example, after the sack of Rome by the barbarian Alaric (A.D. 410), a number of Roman commentators launched an especially significant round of criticisms against Christians. In attempting to explain this traumatic event for the citizens of Rome, the allegedly "eternal" city, they claimed that Constantine's adoption of Christianity had weakened the Roman Empire and made it susceptible to invasion by barbarians. In response to these charges, Christian writers like Orosius, Salvian, and Augustine penned apologetic works defending not only Christian doctrine but Christian practice.

The most famous of these works was Augustine's *The City of God.* Augustine argued that Christians should not be held accountable for the fall of Rome, because substantial weaknesses of the Roman government were evident before the days of Constantine. Augustine, following Christ's teaching, observed that the church of Christ would always be a mixture of wheat and tares. He appeared less convinced than some of his predecessors that "hypocrites" could be sifted out from the church by means of church discipline.

LESSONS FROM THE EARLY CHURCH

The early church offers several lessons about Christian love and its impostor, hypocrisy. *First, when the teachings of Scripture about Christian unity and the loving of God and neighbor are followed, the Gospel advances rapidly indeed.* Nonbelievers could see for themselves the mark of Jesus upon some believers; these Christians did love their brothers and sisters in Christ and prayed for their enemies. Little wonder that later Christians like Spener referred to this era as an illustration of a time when many Christians manifestly lived under the power of the Holy Spirit.

Second, hypocrisy cannot be dismissed as a trifling matter. In his *Justification Reader* (Eerdmans, 2002), Thomas Oden has reiterated that the early Christians did believe in justification by faith alone. Nonetheless, they did not generally permit this doctrine to become a warrant for ethical laxity. On the contrary, the early Christians placed a great emphasis upon faith generating love, upon the maintenance of high ethical standards, upon the avoidance of sexual immorality, upon the keeping of promises, upon the caring for widows and children and the poor— that is, upon doing what is right. Candidates for baptism were to renounce the world and the devil as a sign of their desire to follow Christ alone. If a person were deemed a "hypocrite," many Christians thought the person not a true believer. If a person denied Christ during persecution, he or she often found it difficult to gain readmission to the churches.

Third, one must distinguish between true Christians and hypocrites— as the early Christians readily did—*in order to properly assess a number of atrocities* in the history of the West. Critics allege that many atrocities were perpetrated by hypocritical "Christians"; yet not everyone who bore the name of Christian in Western history and committed a crime was in fact a Christian. When critics cite the excesses of the crusaders, for example, they join in their rebuke a number of Christians of the Middle Ages, who likewise criticized the excesses of the crusaders. This distinction between true Christians and "hypocritical" Christians is not an artificial distinction concocted as a dodge to fend off critics' charges. Christ did teach that not everyone who named His name was in fact a true follower. There are in fact tares among the wheat.

Western Christendom has been the home for countless numbers of people who wore their Christianity lightly, more as a concession to community traditions than out of heartfelt conviction. They were cultural Christians, not heartfelt believers. Many responsible historians have argued, for example, that the so-called "religious" or confessional wars were motivated in part by the economic or dynastic aspirations of the combatants and not solely by any concern for pure doctrine. Likewise, historians know that mixed motives drove the European conquest of the Americas with its bloody excesses. Raw economic incentives and the quest for glory inflamed some explorers, even though they placed their efforts under the flag of Christian monarchs. Still others who were Christians did not live up to Christ's standards in the treatment of native peoples.

HYPOCRISY AND CONTEMPORARY AMERICAN EVANGELICALISM

George Barna, the well respected pollster, has roundly criticized evangelical Christians for their failure to live up to their high calling as the followers of Jesus Christ: "At the risk of sounding like an alarmist, I believe the Church in America has no more than five years—perhaps even less—to turn itself around and begin to affect the culture, rather than be affected by it. Because . . . our central moral and spiritual trends are engulfed in downward spiral, we have no more than a half-decade to turn things around."[8]

If Barna's unforgiving indictment is even partially accurate, then the evangelical community has been engulfed in a massive round of hypocrisy; that is, it does not practice what it preaches. According to Barna, evangelical Christians violate Christian standards of morality as regularly as those who are non-Christian. This makes them hypocrites of the first order.

By contrast, Christian Smith, a sociologist at the University of North Carolina, indicated that the evangelical movement at the beginning of the new millennium was the most vital Christian movement in the United States. In *American Evangelicalism* he wrote "Contemporary American Evangelicalism is thriving. It is more than alive and well. Indeed, . . . it appears to be the strongest of the major Christian traditions in the United States." Smith reported that evangelical laypersons have the highest commitment to traditional orthodox doctrines among self-proclaimed Christians: "Fully ninety-seven percent of evangelicals believe the Bible is God-inspired and without error, a larger number than even that of the fundamentalists." Fully 96 percent of evangelicals believe that a person is saved through "faith in Christ alone." Moreover, Smith indicated that evangelicals practice what they preach: "In keeping with all of our findings thus far about religious strength, the evidence suggests that it is the evangelicals who are most walking their talk."[9]

If George Barna's representation is accurate, non-Christian critics have a persuasive set of data to bolster the hypocrisy charge against evangelicals. By contrast, if Smith's analysis is correct, evangelicals can rejoice that they are generally "walking the talk."

Who is right, Barna or Smith? Professor Smith reminds us that many Christians have had an inner transformation that affects their outward conduct. Yet whether hypocrisy prevails or is the exception, it is true that sometimes we in contemporary American evangelicalism say to unbelievers, "Do not look at us; look at Christ for your example."

In one sense, our admonition has biblical warrant and represents wise counsel. We are to look to Christ, the author and finisher of our faith as our example. But if our counsel represents a clever dodge to justify an accommodating attitude toward sin, then our admonition signals a different stance than many early Christians took. What we are really saying is this: Do not look at us, given our deficient Christian lifestyles. This approach is a far cry from the practice of the early Christians who challenged critics to examine the way they lived as followers of Christ. These early Christians apparently had far less tolerance for hypocrisy than we as American evangelicals countenance.

If a major discrepancy does exist between how we as evangelicals live and what we profess, then we make plausible non-Christians' criticism that Christians are generally hypocrites. Like Jacob Spener's contemporaries, we may have rightly emphasized the doctrine of justification of faith alone but identified that faith with "fleshly illusions." We may have failed to acknowledge Christ's teaching that a good tree bears good fruit.

Certainly the Bible does teach that we are justified by faith alone, through grace alone, through Christ alone. Bible believers should never equivocate for a moment on this doctrine. Works play no role in our salvation. Indeed the first "good work" is to believe on Christ. Moreover, Christ indicates that without Him we can do nothing.

At the same time, Christ also calls upon His disciples through the power of the Holy Spirit to do what He commands. If we have no interest whatsoever in obeying Him, then we should examine ourselves to see if we are in the faith. Luther put the matter this way: "Good works proceed logically from a godly and good person. It is as Christ said: 'An evil tree bears no good fruit, a good tree bears no evil fruit.'" Luther also observed: "All good things come to us from Christ, who has received us into His own life as if He had been what we are. From us they should flow to those who are in need of them. . . . From all the foregoing, the conclusion follows that a Christian lives not in himself, but in Christ and his neighbor; in Christ by faith and in his neighbor by love." Luther knew very well that a mark of the Christian is love.

HOW THEN SHOULD WE LIVE?

Recognize Any Hypocrisy

How then should we live in today's world where we are called hypocrites? First, we should not dismiss hypocrisy charges with disdain but consider them with a humble spirit. It is very easy for us to be hypo-critical. Given our twisted motivations, we can be hypocritical in gen-uinely creative ways. Charles Spurgeon cites an insightful letter from a Dr. Payson on this point:

> My parish as well as my heart, very much resembles the garden of the sluggard and, what is worse, I find that very many of my desires for the melioration of both proceed either from pride or vanity or indolence. I look at the weeds which overspread my garden, and breathe out an earnest wish that they were eradicated. But why? What prompts the wish? It may be that I may walk out and say to myself, 'In what fine or-der is my garden kept!' This is *pride.* Or, it may be that my neighbors may look over the wall and say, 'How finely your garden flourishes!' This is *vanity.* Or, I may wish for the destruction of the weeds, just because I am tired of pulling them up. This is *indolence.*[10]

It is so, then, that our desire for holiness could be tainted by evil mo-tives. For us to avoid hypocrisy and live holy lives, we desperately need the Holy Spirit's power.

If particular charges of hypocrisy that critics raise against us are valid, then we need to turn away from whatever is hypocritical. We need to confess whatever constitutes a discrepancy between scriptural teaching and what we do. If the hypocrisy involves known sins, we should con-fess them and make restitution when necessary. If we have been hypo-critical in denying Christ when we are around our non-Christian friends, we should go back to them and "deny our denials." We are taught to live with a good conscience before God and before all other people (see 1 Timothy 1:5), including the household of faith. If some of our prob-lems are related to addictions, we may need to seek the help of caring Christian friends, pastors, or professional counselors.

Given our old sin nature, we will find it very difficult to refrain from being hypocritical if we depend on our own strength and not the Lord's grace and power. Our chief motivation as Christians should be to please our Lord and Savior, Jesus Christ, and to bring glory to Him. If we are inveterate hypocrites, neither our worship nor our service will please our God. The mark of the Christian upon us will be largely invisible.

Even if we do sense that, through the leading of the Holy Spirit, "we walk in the light" (we confess our sins daily and enjoy fellowship with other Christians and with God, per 1 John 1), we may still become the target of a false accusation of hypocrisy. As noted previously, in today's world, to believe that Jesus Christ is "the way and the truth and the life" is sufficient to gain that reproach. If such occurs, we should guard against letting malice toward our critics fester in our hearts. We are to love our enemies.

Answer the Misrepresentations

Second, we should consider more directly the question of whether we will remain silent and let "unfair criticisms" from the larger culture about Christian faith and practice go unchallenged. Should we, like Justin Martyr or Augustine or Calvin or John Wesley, answer more serious misrepresentations? If we do not respond to critics' charges, we risk letting the charges take on a life of their own. These charges may possibly become assumptions that can feed anti-Christian sentiments in the culture at large.

At the same time, if we try to answer the critics' concerns, we can risk becoming consumed in a sectarian spirit, exhibiting an unseemly militancy in an attempt to win arguments at any cost. Jacob Spener's wise counsel remains pertinent: "Don't stake everything on argument."

A balanced, Holy Spirit–empowered approach is essential here. Francis Schaeffer, for example, was perfectly willing to engage in debate in defense of the Christian faith. At the same time, he took great pains to treat opponents with love, dignity, and respect. As he bore the mark of the Christian, he often retained the possibility of witnessing to his opponent during or after the debate.

If we write cultural apologetics for the Christian faith (that is, a defense of Christianity's truth claims as well as the ethics and values it teaches), we may want to remember that no guarantees exist that "success" will greet our efforts. Even if we use measured arguments, our

readers may not be convinced by what we say. God the Holy Spirit converts people to Christ. We do not. Rather, we are called to be faithful
in our work of glorifying God.

This said, there are a number of issues evangelical writers could prof-
itably tackle. For example, in greater Chicago, the public editor of the
Chicago Tribune has invited those who think the media is "pro-gay" to
present arguments sufficiently persuasive that the media will think they
should be published: "They need to persuade us in the media to put their
arguments into the public arena."

Besides writing on this important topic, we need careful studies directed to the general public that will help make it clear that not all atrocities attributed to people who called themselves "Christians" in Western
history were performed by true disciples of Christ. This distinction,
one made by Jesus Himself, needs to be unpacked with no special plead-
ing and in a persuasive and non-defensive fashion so that a talented
columnist like Molly Ivins, cited earlier, will understand that her analysis about the hypocrisy of Christians should be revised. We may wring
our hands about the unfairness of comments she made, but she probably proposed them having never read a persuasive rejoinder to her familiar litany of charges.

Participate in the Public Debate

Third, the Christian community needs to be active in the public
square, participating in national discussion. We need careful studies to
explain the reasons it is not hypocritical for Christians to take stands
regarding public policy—stands that are informed by religious values.
An emerging literature exists that helps make the case in a convincing
fashion. For example, in a remarkable article, "The Wall That Never
Was," Hugh Heclo argues that the Founding Fathers never intended to
create a wall between church and state of the sort imagined by many
jurists today. He presents powerful reasons it is so important to have a
"religious outlook" influence our public life.[11] What adds persuasiveness
to his proposal is his acknowledgment that careful safeguards should be

provided to block any form of a religious takeover of the state that would result in the cessation or loss of civil rights for those who are not religious.

We need studies that explain that "living well" and true "happiness" flow from following and obeying Christian teachings. Long ago, Jonathan Edwards noted that we were made by our Creator to live according to His divine directives. If we rebel against these directives, we will be miserable. No matter how wealthy or famous we may become, we will not experience "living well."

THE HAPPIEST PEOPLE

Christians, then, can be the happiest people in the world despite trying circumstances. Charles Spurgeon described well the joy that filled his own soul: "When the Lord first pardoned my sin, I was so joyous that I could scarcely refrain from dancing. On the road home from the house where I had been set free, I wanted to shout in the street the story of my deliverance. My soul was so happy that I wanted to tell every snowflake that was falling from heaven of the wondrous love of Jesus who had blotted out the sins of my most rebellious nature. But it is not only at the beginning of the Christian life that believers have a reason to sing; as long as they live they discover reasons to sing about the ways of the Lord, and their experiences of His constant loving-kindness lead them to say, 'I will extol the LORD at all times; His praise will always be on my lips.'"[12]

At the same time, Christians caught up in hypocrisy or rebellion can be genuinely miserable people. For them, experiencing the very real joys of righteous living is at best a faded memory.

With all these things in mind, "how then should we live?" Not as hypocrites but rather as forgiven sinners depending daily upon the Holy Spirit's power in every aspect of our lives.

What's in a Name

Are We All Fundamentalists?

Who are the Fundamentalists and Should We Fear
Them?" In the mid-1980s, those two provocative questions headlined a
brochure for an adult Sunday school class at a suburban mainline church
near Chicago. The leaders of the class calculated that the advertisement
might catch parishioners' attention. They were right. The attendance
at the four-week series was substantial. Apparently by the mid-1980s,
fears about "fundamentalists" had become sufficiently elevated among
certain churchgoers that the series' title with its ominous overtones in-
trigued them.

In interacting with one of the series speakers, however, several attendees indicated that they did not actually "fear" fundamentalists. Their
interest in the topic was born more of general curiosity about the nature of American fundamentalism. A few volunteered they had enjoyed
friendly relations with people who called themselves fundamentalists.

They viewed these people as generous and kind. Others acknowledged that they had once been fundamentalists but now embraced a more liberal form of Christianity.

Most of these individuals who had some familiarity with fundamentalism associated the movement with theologically conservative American Protestants, who practiced "strict" lifestyles. They said that the fundamentalists they knew opposed "worldliness." The fundamentalists did not attend movies and dances, did not smoke cigarettes, gamble, or drink alcoholic beverages. The fundamentalists believed the Bible was literally true; it was the Word of God and inerrant (without errors).

Still others attendees who had little firsthand acquaintance with fundamentalism confessed a sense of anxiety about fundamentalists. They wanted to know how the teachers of the class would respond to the specific question, *Should the class members fear American fundamentalists?* By the mid-1980s, the media's increasing identification of the word *fundamentalism* with Muslim extremists had apparently stoked worries in their minds about any fundamentalist group, whether its members were American Protestants or advocates of another world religion.

Today, if leaders of an adult Sunday school class in a mainline church announced a similar series devoted to fundamentalism, the majority of attendees would probably assume their teacher was going to offer a comparative study of various religious fundamentalisms from around the world. This more wide-ranging approach for studying fundamentalism has now become commonplace in religious studies programs and in certain church circles. In this framework American Christian fundamentalism is treated as only one example among various world fundamentalisms.

MODERN IMAGES OF THE FUNDAMENTALIST

Since the early 1980s a remarkable transformation of the definitions and connotations of the word *fundamentalism* has taken place in the United States and throughout the world. Now many people do fear religious people if they are depicted as fundamentalists, whether American or otherwise. The word *fundamentalist* can evoke images of crazed religious fanatics who are intolerant of the religious beliefs of others and intent upon forcing their views upon other peoples.

From CNN cable television and international news agencies to editorialists at leading newspapers and distinguished authors of books comparing world religions, many gatekeepers of the culture at large have reinforced this stereotypical image by making repeated allusions to religious extremists as fundamentalists—perpetrators of acts of terror in the name of their god.

In a recent article entitled "Islamic Scholar Takes on Fundamentalists," *Chicago Tribune* national correspondent Vincent J. Schodolski described the threats that Haled Abou El Fadl, a professor of Islamic law at UCLA, had experienced due to his criticisms of "Islamic fundamentalism." According to the professor, a particular form of Islam called wahhabism was a virulent source of the radical militancy among Muslim extremists. He argued that wahhabism betrayed the Koran's teaching that "if you are harsh and unkind, people will not come to you, so the Koran recognizes that decency has to be there." For making this claim and others, Haled Abou El Fadl received multiple threats.

Schodolski's article, following the professor's lead, did not hesitate to compare wahhabism, the extremist form of Islam, to American fundamentalism: "That form of Islam, known as wahhabism, is in some ways similar to fundamentalist views in Christianity and Judaism." The editors of the *Tribune* apparently approved the author's linkage of these groups—even with the linkage's negative entailments for Christian fundamentalists and conservative Jews.[1]

Not only do the media and many academics use the expression *fundamentalism* in this fashion, evangelical Christians often do as well. Now, obviously, a certain tension exists for many Christians when they employ the word in this way. Most know that the original fundamentalists were conservative American Protestants who largely ignored denominational distinctives and came together to defend what they perceived to be fundamental Christian beliefs under attack from Protestant modernists. Nonetheless, evangelical Christians sometimes use the word *fundamentalist* in referring to "militant" followers of other world religions. In evangelical debates the term is also sometimes used as a pejorative epithet to designate those conservative Protestants who uphold biblical inerrancy, even if these people call themselves evangelicals.

Analyzing the various ways Christians and others have used the word *fundamentalist* from its first principal appearance in 1920 through the transformation of its connotations in the early 1980s might at first resemble a detour that takes us far away from our quest to understand better what it means to bear the mark of Jesus. Nonetheless, this kind of reflection is necessary. If we hope the world will ever see the mark of Jesus upon us, they must have a sense that we are after all authentic Christians and not simply militant religious ideologues. The careless application of the word *fundamentalist* to believers attempting to uphold the fundamentals of the faith can hinder non-Christians from seeing the mark of Jesus upon them.

NO DISTINCTION

If non-Christians are predisposed to think that evangelical Christians bear traits characteristic of what they construe as an ideological fundamentalism—tendencies toward violence, intolerance, and bigotry—which are at odds with teachings about love and respect of one's neighbor—they may be very dismissive of our Gospel message.

Evangelical Christians who don't regard themselves as fundamentalists may conclude they will escape any negative entailments of association with so-called worldwide fundamentalisms. Unfortunately, a number of secular persons in the media have little interest in the carefully designated distinctions that we believe permit us to say we are evangelicals and not fundamentalists. From their point of view, our denials notwithstanding, evangelicals are fundamentalists.

Why is this? For them, any person who says that Jesus Christ is *the* way, *the* truth, and *the* life—who believes that Christ is the only way of salvation—warrants the description *fundamentalist*. To many, *fundamentalism* serves as an appropriate code word connoting the intolerance and religious bigotry of those who make the exclusivist claim that salvation comes only through Jesus Christ. Because evangelical Christians do in fact affirm this central Christian belief, they may find themselves suddenly labeled as fundamentalists. Critics often ignore the claim of notable evangelical Christians that no contradictions exist between affirming that Christ is the only way of salvation and sincerely defending the rights of conscience of those who hold other religious or secular beliefs.

Given this perception of fundamentalism in corners of the secular world, the question, *Are we all fundamentalists?* may possess greater relevance to the effectiveness of our Christian witness than we may have first supposed.

Kenneth Kantzer, one of the most well-respected evangelical theologians of the twentieth century, was asked on occasion whether he was a fundamentalist. He would inevitably reply: "What do you mean by the word? If you mean someone who upholds the fundamentals of the faith, then I am a fundamentalist. But if you mean someone who looks down on the life of the mind or would impose religious convictions through forms of coercion upon another, I am by no means a fundamentalist."

A BRIEF HISTORY OF AMERICAN FUNDAMENTALISM

To answer inquiries about whether we are all fundamentalists, we need to have at least some understanding of the history of American fundamentalism. For starters, we need to know that the goals and thinking of fundamentalists have changed over time. Fundamentalists of the 1920s, for example, initially wanted to stay within the mainline denominations, whereas many fundamentalists post-1957 had not only separated from mainline denominations but were critical of Christians like Billy Graham who advocated "cooperative evangelism" with mainline churches. We need to know what distinguishes the Christian faith from other world religions to help others avoid placing the people who uphold and defend Christian fundamentals in the same group with individuals who espouse hostile ideological and religious beliefs. Such clumping together is neither helpful nor fair-minded. As we shall see, Peter Berger, one of the world's leading sociologists of religion, has raised serious objections to this kind of categorizing.

Our survey of the history of fundamentalism will be necessarily brief and impressionistic. Nonetheless, it may help us sense more fully the import of the question, *Are we all fundamentalists?* Our review should also make clear that secular and evangelical scholars who link American fundamentalists to traits assumed characteristic of worldwide fundamentalisms should reconsider making this linkage. While several shared traits may at first seem to link these groups, the differences between the core beliefs and actions of American fundamentalists of whatever timeframe and the beliefs and actions of religious fanatics who kill in the name of their god are too great to make the movements genuinely similar.

"NON-SEPARATING" FUNDAMENTALISM: 1919–1937

The Fundamentalist/Modernist Controversy

After World War I, a major battle (long in the making) known as the fundamentalist/modernist controversy broke out for the control of a number of northern Protestant denominations, especially the Northern Baptist Convention and the Northern Presbyterian Church. In his famous sermon "Shall the Fundamentalists Win?" (1922) Harry Emerson Fosdick fired one of the early major salvos of the struggle. A gifted speaker, Fosdick, a Protestant liberal, declared: "The present world situation smells to heaven! And now, in the presence of colossal problems, which must be solved in Christ's name and for Christ's sake, the fundamentalists propose to drive from the Christian churches all the consecrated souls who do not agree with their theory of inspiration [of the Bible]."[2] Fosdick assured his listeners the fundamentalists would not win.

Elsewhere, he advocated modernism: "It is primarily an adaptation, an adjustment, an accommodation of the Christian faith to contemporary scientific thinking. . . . It is started by taking the intellectual culture of a particular period as its criterion and then adjusting Christian teaching to that standard."[3]

The fundamentalist/modernist controversy, then, pitted theological conservatives who wanted to uphold the fundamentals of the Christian faith against theological liberals who wanted to accommodate Christianity to the findings of "modern knowledge," especially findings from higher criticism of the Bible and Darwin's theory of evolution. A number of Protestant denominations and ethnic churches did not participate in the battle.

In a 1920 article of the *Watchman-Examiner,* Curtis Lee Laws, the magazine's editor, provided what became a standard description of those people on the fundamentalist side of the controversy.

> We here and now move that a new word be adopted to describe the men among us who insist that the landmarks should not be removed. "Conservatives" is too closely allied with reactionary forces in all walks of life. "Premillennialists" is too closely allied with a single doctrine and not sufficiently inclusive. "Landmarkers" has a historical disadvantage and connotes a particular group of radical conservatives. We suggest that those who still cling to the great fundamentals and who mean to do battle royal for the fundamentals should be called "fundamentalists."[4]

Laws' definition emphasized the point that fundamentalists believed they were conservative Protestant Christians who were clinging to "the great fundamentals" of the Christian faith and prepared to "battle" for them.

What Are the Fundamentals?

While conservative Protestants generally upheld most of the same "great fundamentals," their lists of these doctrines did not always fully overlap. Differing notions of which beliefs constituted the nonnegotiable fundamentals help explain the presence of various groups of fundamentalists in the 1920s and their doctrinal emphases in relation to their confessional allies, Pentecostals and others. Confessional Presbyterians, for example, at their general assemblies (1910, 1916, 1923) approved five doctrines as "essential and necessary," or nonnegotiable: (1) the inerrancy of Scripture in the original documents; (2) Christ's virgin birth; (3) Christ's vicarious atonement; (4) Christ's bodily resurrection; and (5) the reality of biblical miracles. These Presbyterians acknowledged that their relatively short list did not exhaust the number of important orthodox Christian doctrines.

By contrast, The World's Christian Fundamentals Association meeting in 1919 affirmed nine essential doctrines. While embracing the same doctrines noted by the Presbyterians, they added the "personal, premillennial and imminent return of our Lord and Savior Jesus Christ" [article VII], an eschatological belief not acceptable to many confessional Presbyterians who were amillenarian (stressing the present Kingdom of God in which Christ rules the earth) or postmillenarian (believing Christ will return after the millennium) in eschatology. But the next year (1920), Curtis Lee Laws did not include premillennialism in his definition of a fundamentalist.

For his part, James M. Gray, the president of Moody Bible Institute and a dispensational premillennialist, wondered about the value of using the term *fundamentalist.* In a response (1922) to Dr. Harry Emerson Fosdick's sermon "Shall the Fundamentalists Win?" Gray wrote: "I do not call myself a fundamentalist, not because I lack sympathy with the Bible truths for which that name now stands, but because I think the name itself is unnecessary and perhaps undesirable." Gray thought it was unnecessary to coin a term to replace the time-honored expression "the evangelical faith" that he identified with the "faith once delivered." He feared that a new name would permit opponents "to speak of fundamentalism as something new, and not only new but divisive in the churches which are said to be already 'sufficiently split and riven.'"[5]

For their part, most Pentecostals like Bishop Hilary King of the Pentecostal/Holiness Church affirmed the same Christian beliefs as the confessional Presbyterians and fundamentalists, including justification by faith alone and the inerrancy of Scripture, but noted other fundamental doctrines they believed indispensable for a vital Christian faith. In addition, many African-American Christians upheld the same core beliefs of other Protestants but found themselves separated from whites by longstanding issues related to racial prejudice and economic and social inequalities.

Despite disagreements, especially regarding issues of eschatology and what constituted an appropriate Christian lifestyle, fundamentalists and confessional Christians in particular sometimes worked together against a common foe, Protestant liberals. Many fundamentalists admired the theological acumen of the Princeton Seminary professor J. Gresham Machen, a Presbyterian clergyman. In the eyes of the media, Machen represented the leading intellectual among fundamentalists, although the Princeton professor would only reluctantly refer to himself as a fundamentalist.

Machen, a confessional Christian, was by no means favorably disposed toward the premillennial eschatology of his fundamentalist allies. Nonetheless, he believed these colleagues upheld the essentials of the faith, like biblical inerrancy. In *Christianity and Liberalism* (Eerdmans, 1923), Machen wrote: "Their error [of believing in the premillennial return of Christ], serious though it may be, is not deadly error; and Christian fellowship, with loyalty not only to the Bible but to the creeds of the Church, can still unite us with them." Likewise, Machen believed Anglicans were mistaken in their views of church governance and Arminians erred in their anthropology. But once again, Machen recognized members of both groups as true Christians, whereas he portrayed Protestant liberals quite bluntly as naturalists, the followers of an entirely different religion than Christianity.

Machen explained the principle he followed in cooperating with other Christians even though he did not endorse all of their doctrinal distinctives: "We do not mean, in insisting upon the doctrinal basis of Christianity, that all points of doctrine are equally important. It is perfectly possible for Christian fellowship to be maintained despite differences of opinion."[6]

In many regards Machen's stance resembled the general inclusivist principle behind "The Fundamentals, A Testimony to the Truth" (1910–1915), a series of pamphlets that had appeared in the decade before Christianity and liberalism and the product of biblical scholars and theologians from both the United States and the United Kingdom. More than two million copies of these pamphlets defending the evangelical faith and challenging Protestant liberalism were distributed free of charge throughout the English-speaking world to pastors, Christian workers, and YMCA and YWCA leaders. Two wealthy businessmen, the Stewart brothers, funded the enterprise.

The Debate Engaged

By the time Machen penned *Christianity and Liberalism*, the appearance of Fosdick's provocative sermon in 1922 made it clear that the publication of "The Fundamentals" had not stemmed the theological tide. Conservative Protestants no longer seemed to believe they could win their engagement with Protestant liberals with serene discourse and rational argument. Instead they used the war analogy in describing their struggle to wrest the control of the Northern Baptist Convention and the Northern Presbyterian Church from the control of Protestant liberals. Curtis Laws noted that a fundamentalist not only upheld the fundamentals of the faith but was willing to do "battle royal" for them. "Militancy," or the willingness to battle for the faith in denominational disputes, became a trait of early "fundamentalists."

In a similar fashion, by the early 1920s Machen resorted to "battle" vocabulary to describe the conflict in which conservative Protestants were engaged. He provided his perception of the high stakes in the contest: "In the sphere of religion . . . the present time is a time of conflict; the great redemptive religion which has always been known as Christianity is battling against a totally diverse type of religious belief, which is only the more destructive because it makes use of traditional Christian terminology." He believed that he and his conservative colleagues were caught up in a life-and-death theological struggle with Protestant liberals or modernists over cardinal doctrines of the Christian faith, not secondary beliefs.

At the beginning of the conflict, the conservatives entertained hopes that they might still force Protestant liberals out of key denominations. But as the 1920s wore on, it became clear that the conservative Protestants whom Machen called "evangelicals" had failed to force liberals out of the denominations. Consequently, many conservatives began to think that Machen's second option, the creation of new denominations and churches, was the only alternative left to them. Independent churches and new conservative denominations were birthed. Other conservative and moderate Protestants decided to stay within the denominations.

Setbacks for Conservatives

In 1929, Machen, having lost his attempt to keep Princeton Theological Seminary in the hands of Presbyterian conservatives, left the school along with a number of other faculty and students and established Westminster Theological Seminary. Six years later, Machen was put on trial by the Northern Presbyterian Church for his refusal to disband the Independent Board of Foreign Missions, an agency he had formed to funnel monies to conservative Presbyterian missionaries overseas. Found guilty at the trial, he lost his right to minister in the denomination. Soon after, he helped establish the Orthodox Presbyterian Church.

In the culture at large, the Scopes trial (or "Monkey Trial") of 1925 featured the fundamentalist politician William Jennings Bryan dueling the famous trial lawyer Clarence Darrow. The trial ostensibly centered on charges against John Scopes, who had violated a Tennessee law by teaching evolution in a high school. The American Civil Liberties Union (ACLU) and others had in fact manufactured the Scopes' case to test the validity of the state law and to put Dayton, Tennessee, on the map. Scopes was found guilty. Nonetheless, many Americans who followed Darrow's browbeating questioning of Bryan regarding the dating of creation emerged with the impression that the Bible should not be viewed as a reliable source of information for a "scientific" understanding of the natural world, or at least that Bryan's interpretation of the Bible was not credible.

At the conclusion of the Scopes trial, many critics believed that fundamentalists were not only anti-intellectual in not accepting the advances of science, but that they were also attempting to foist their religious values upon American education, ignoring the separation of church and state. Bryan's actual position was more sophisticated than that; he in fact did not want tax money "to propagate a creed [evolution] or deny a faith," as one contemporary explained his position.

Even though William Jennings Bryan's death soon after the trial created much sympathy for him personally, and Darrow's baiting cross-examination techniques made ACLU leaders wary of claiming a public relations victory at Dayton, the result was a growing perception that

Christians were not able to answer proponents of evolutionary theory backed by science.

Other issues also affected negatively the general fundamentalist cause. Revivalism, so closely associated with evangelicalism in the nineteenth century, came under stinging criticism. Sinclair Lewis's book *Elmer Gantry* (1927), with its portrayal of a conniving, womanizing evangelist, did much to discredit evangelists and revivals. Critics railed at evangelist Billy Sunday's tent meetings in which people "hit the sawdust trail" up the aisle during an altar call. Protestant liberals often looked to education as a way to "nurture" and "Christianize" the young and turned their backs on revivals and "conversions." Some religious leaders thought a child should never know a time when he or she was not a Christian and thus had no need of a "conversion."

By 1933, the crusade of many Baptists and Methodists to uphold prohibition had ended in failure with the repeal of the Eighteenth Amendment. Historian Sydney Ahlstrom has suggested that this defeat contributed to a growing lack of confidence among Protestants that they could affect the morals of the nation. Like other Americans, they sometimes felt that the country's social and economic problems were so great that only the federal government (and not the churches) could possibly address them.

The influence of fundamentalists and their confessional allies like Machen upon American religion now seemed greatly diminished, the apparent victory of Protestant liberals in a number of key northern denominations secure.

Many of these early fundamentalists, then, were ecumenically oriented conservative Protestants who wanted to purify their denominations from within. Setting aside denominational differences, they came together around the historic "fundamental" doctrines of the Christian church. Some of these conservative Protestants who called themselves fundamentalists identified dispensational premillennial eschatology as a "fundamental" of the faith; other fundamentalists did not. A number of leading Presbyterian and Pentecostal pastors affirmed dispensational theology as well.

These early fundamentalists often served Christ faithfully and at great personal sacrifice on the mission field and in churches and city missions in the United States. Their personal ethics were quite "pietistic." They viewed attendance at movies, dancing, gambling, and the drinking of alcoholic beverages as forms of "worldliness" that violated biblical teaching. Confessional Christians like Machen did not always share these same standards of piety.

On January 1, 1937, J. Gresham Machen succumbed to a bout of pneumonia while on a preaching mission in the upper Midwest. His passing appeared to mark the end of a significant phase of the fundamentalist/ modernist controversy.

Setbacks for Liberals

Though they had defeated conservative, confessional Presbyterians in Northern Presbyterianism and conservative Northern Baptists, Protestant liberals experienced setbacks themselves as the 1930s wound down. The message of Protestant liberalism was not an easy one to promote during the Depression because "things did not seem to be getting better and better as mankind evolved." In 1935, Harry Emerson Fosdick indicated, "We must go beyond modernism." The advance of Japanese armies in China, the rise of the Nationalist Socialists in Germany, and rumors of the persecution of Jews dispelled thoughts that the "Great War" was the last war.

With setbacks experienced by both conservative and liberal Protestants, the influence of Protestantism itself to affect the values of the nation dropped off substantially. Earlier in the 1920s, Reinhold Niebuhr astutely observed: "The secularization of modern life is partly due to the advance of science, but also the moral inadequacies of Protestantism. If liberal Protestantism is too pantheistic, traditional Protestantism is too quietistic to meet the moral problems of a socially complex age."[7]

SEPARATIST FUNDAMENTALISM AND THE EMERGENCE OF THE "NEW EVANGELICAL" MOVEMENT (1937–1957)

As self-designated fundamentalists emerged from the 1930s, they often carried with them the heavy baggage of an unfavorable reputation.

Protestant liberals castigated them for their alleged anti-intellectualism, their belief in biblical inerrancy, their supposed use of a "literal hermeneutic," their apparent lack of concern for social action, their individualistic "pietistic" ethics, and their continued practice of revivalism. More moderate fundamentalists wondered if their movement's infighting and militancy served as a millstone holding back the advance of the Gospel in the United States. Confessional Protestants like Missouri Synod Lutherans disliked the fundamentalists' apparent lack of appreciation for Christian creeds and sacraments, or ordinances.

In the 1940s, a number of fundamentalists interpreted these criticisms as indications that the critics themselves had no intention of following the clear teachings of Scripture about how Christians should live, think, and maintain personal purity while facing the temptations of "worldliness" and religious formalism. A commitment to separatism in the name of doctrinal and moral purity became an even more dominant characteristic of one wing of the fundamentalist movement. Separatism now included not only breaking with doctrinally compromised denominations but breaking with "moderate" fundamentalists and others, soon to be known as the "new evangelicals." In 1941 Carl T. McIntire, who like Machen had been removed from the Northern Presbyterian Church, formed the American Council of Christian Churches, a group of believers committed to upholding the purity of the faith.

The next year, 1942–1943, a group of more moderate fundamentalists, evangelicals, confessional Christians (including the Christian Reformed Church), Salvation Army, and Pentecostals joined together to create the National Association of Evangelicals (NAE). These Christians wanted to uphold the fundamentals of the faith while avoiding the more negative traits associated with the fundamentalist movement. In "The Unvoiced Multitudes," Harold Ockenga, one of the principal founders of NAE, set forth his vision:

> I believe we must first of all seek unity. This means that this millstone of rugged independency which has held back innumerable movements before, in which individual leaders must be the whole hog or none, must be utterly repudiated by every one of us. A terrible indictment may be laid

against fundamentalism because of its failures, divisions, and controversies. This must be admitted by those of us who believe in the fundamentals and who also seek a new outlook. . . . The division is no longer between denominations; the division is between those who believe in Christ and the Bible, and those who reject Christ—the Christ of the cross and the Bible. . . . It is folly to speak of the union of the true Church and then declare that those who profess to believe in the doctrines of the true Church can never work in unity.[8]

Ockenga hoped that evangelicals would penetrate centers of higher education, the boardrooms of business, and halls of government with the Gospel. At the same time, he was worried about the advance of Roman Catholicism and secularism in the United States.

Many conservative Christians began to rally to Ockenga's vision. By the late 1940s, they more frequently identified themselves as evangelicals than as fundamentalists. In the same time frame, however, confessional believers like the Christian Reformed Church withdrew from NAE, and some Pentecostals formed their own group.

In 1947, Carl F. H. Henry (1913–2003) published *The Uneasy Conscience of Modern Fundamentalism* (foreword written by Harold Ockenga), in which he noted that although fundamentalists had rightly upheld the fundamentals of the faith, they had not sufficiently emphasized the Bible's teachings about social justice and corporate ethics. The fundamentalists were forfeiting a hearing for the Gospel because they seemed not sufficiently concerned about changing or improving the lot of the oppressed and about political and social engagement.

It should be remembered that in the 1940s the distinctions between fundamentalists and evangelicals were not especially clear-cut. Many of the conservative Protestants who worked together in creating large numbers of the nondenominational "parachurch" organizations could interchangeably call themselves fundamentalists or evangelicals.

Historian Joel Carpenter has recounted the story of the stunning rebuilding of conservative Protestantism that began in the 1930s and continued through the "Post World War II Awakening" until 1957. Radio ministries like Charles Fuller's "Old-Fashioned Revival Hour,"

Walter A. Maier's "Lutheran Hour"; youth ministries like Youth for Christ, Young Life, Navigators and Word of Life, InterVarsity, and later Campus Crusade for Christ (1951); the creation of new mission agencies; the founding of many Bible schools and Fuller Theological Seminary (1947)—all of these bolstered and encouraged these conservative Protestants, who often viewed themselves as outsiders to the American religious establishment, controlled by the leaders of mainline denominations.

During the same decade, young scholars at Harvard and Boston University, including Edward J. Carnell, Kenneth Kantzer, Samuel Schultz, and Carl Henry, studied with the goal of improving the quality of education among conservative Protestants. Their studies presaged the waves of young evangelicals who would decide to pursue a career in academics, offsetting the anti-intellectual stereotype weighing heavily on the reputation of conservative Christians.

With evangelist Billy Graham's rise to national prominence in the Los Angeles Revival of 1949, conservative Protestants had one of their own who could speak for them with the nation's politicians and religious leaders. At the London Crusade in 1954, Billy Graham became an international figure. Thousands upon thousands of people around the world came to know Christ as Lord and Savior through Graham's faithful preaching of the Gospel. Many Americans viewed him as one of the most respected and beloved persons in the United States. The Graham crusades did much to remove lingering negative memories of Elmer Gantry–style revivalism.

With Billy Graham's backing, in 1956 the magazine *Christianity Today* was launched and provided the evangelical/fundamentalist movement with a respected thought journal read by religious leaders from across the theological spectrum. Leaving his teaching post at Fuller Theological Seminary, Carl Henry gave the young magazine excellent editorial direction. Henry and others believed that America might be on the edge of another Great Awakening.

Yet new divisions among conservative Protestants quickly dispelled these hopes. Billy Graham had adopted "cooperative evangelism" as a strategy for reaching the nation with the Gospel. He invited not only fundamentalist and evangelical churches and groups to support his crusades but mainline denominational churches as well. From Mr. Graham's point of view, this approach involved no compromise of the Gospel. If anyone was compromising, it might be Protestant liberals who agreed to support a Graham crusade. Some of Graham's fundamentalist friends, like evangelists Jack Wyrtzen, John R. Rice, and Bob Jones II, did not see things this way. They thought Billy Graham was compromising clear biblical teaching about biblical separation.

Things came to a head at Billy Graham's Madison Square Garden, New York, Crusade of 1957, when these fundamentalists decided to withdraw their support from his evangelistic efforts, issuing some acrid criticisms. Because Billy Graham had been such a close friend of many of these men and they all shared a sincere commitment to evangelistic outreach ("to see souls saved"), this breakup between them was as poignant as it was painful.

DIVISIONS BETWEEN EVANGELICALS AND SECOND-DEGREE SEPARATIONISTS

In the next decades, a specifically evangelical movement continued to develop among conservative Protestants—whether confessional, charismatic, evangelical, or otherwise—who appreciated the ministry of Billy Graham, *Christianity Today*, and schools like Fuller Theological Seminary and Wheaton College. Harold Ockenga sometimes spoke of this movement as the "new evangelical movement."

Those individuals who criticized Mr. Graham were likewise very critical of the "new evangelicalism," sometimes called "neo-evangelicalism." They viewed themselves as the true fundamentalists who were upholding the purity of the faith and Christian ethics. They wanted to be militant in their defense of right doctrine. Moreover, they viewed individuals who did not separate from Mr. Graham's ministry as theologically compromised.

These fundamentalists, therefore, practiced what was known as "second-degree separation," separating from those who had not separated from Mr. Graham or "new evangelical" institutions. The leaders of this fundamentalist movement included Jack Wyrtzen, Bob Jones II and III, Jerry Falwell, and others. Whereas fundamentalists of the 1920s had desired to remain within the mainline denominations, these fundamentalists pressed the separationist case against the "new evangelicals" and sometimes against other fundamentalists if the latter did not seem separationist enough. A major concern that these fundamentalists had was that the "new evangelicals" would abandon the doctrine of biblical inerrancy, a doctrine earlier fundamentalists and evangelicals had upheld.

A number of fundamentalists thought their prediction that the "new evangelicals" would compromise the faith had been fulfilled when Fuller Theological Seminary changed its statement of faith in the early 1960s. The statement no longer indicated that the Bible is inerrant but rather it is infallible for matters of faith and practice. Scholars at Fuller believed this stance represented the historic position of the Protestant churches and permitted greater freedom in doing biblical criticism and studying science.

In the 1960s and 1970s, cracks within the unity of the "new evangelicalism" began to emerge, with many evangelical groups continuing to uphold biblical inerrancy (for example, the Evangelical Theological Society), whereas other evangelical groups did not. Similar divisions surfaced in the Southern Baptist Convention and among Missouri Synod Lutherans. In the latter churches, full-scale battles for the control of the denominations erupted in the 1970s with the inerrantists generally winning the day by the early 1980s in both instances. In these contests, those disputants who opposed the doctrine of biblical inerrancy sometimes scored their opponents as "fundamentalists." Thus the word could serve as an epithet in debates over biblical inerrancy.

Newsweek magazine declared 1976 "The Year of the Evangelical" after presidential candidate Jimmy Carter had declared he was a "born-again Christian." However, Carl Henry was much less sanguine about the strength of the evangelical movement. In *Evangelicals in Search of Identity,* Henry wrote: "The evangelical movement shows disturbing signs of dissipating its energies and of forfeiting its initiative. . . . The issue of biblical inerrancy is today dividing evangelicals into ever more rigidly competitive camps."[9] Harold Lindsell would later call this competition "The Battle for the Bible" and authored a book by that name. By the early 1980s,

Lindsell thought the "Golden Age" of an evangelicalism that was committed to biblical inerrancy was past.

Whereas evangelical Christians debated among themselves the nature of biblical authority, those persons who were "stricter" fundamentalists struggled with the maintenance of their doctrine of second-degree separation. In the late 1970s, a Gallup Poll suggested that more than fifty million Americans were "born-again Christians"—a sufficient number to claim that they, with their potential nonevangelical allies, represented a majority within American society. In order to define this broad group, Jerry Falwell named them the "Moral Majority"—a group that created consternation among some fundamentalists.

The decision of Mr. Falwell, a gifted evangelist, organizer, and second-degree separationist, to work with non-fundamentalists for a national "moral agenda" displeased many of his second-degree separationist friends. They viewed his actions as an unacceptable violation of the principle of biblical separation and in turn separated from him. At the same time, the Moral Majority engendered in many non-Christians the fear that fundamentalists wanted to impose "Christian" values upon the nation.

As the decade of the 1970s closed, deep divisions within fundamentalism regarding who was actually upholding the purity of the Christian faith in a "separated" way made cooperative efforts difficult among those who called themselves fundamentalists. The movement fractured repeatedly. But it was at least clear that when people spoke about fundamentalists, giving that word various shades of meaning, they were referencing conservative Protestant Christians, not the militant followers of other world religions. For some conservative Christians (approximately four million people, according to researcher John Fea),[10] the word *fundamentalist* represented a badge of honor. They wore it proudly. Other conservative Christians preferred to call themselves other names like evangelicals, charismatics, confessional believers, Bible believers (many African-Americans preferred this term), or to use a derivative of their church's name, such as Presbyterians, Pentecostals, Southern Baptists, Misssouri Synod Lutheran, etc.

THE WORD *FUNDAMENTALIST* AND "MILITANT" FOLLOWERS
OF WORLD RELIGIONS (1980–2000)

In 1980, leading scholars and writers for the media began to make the case for the existence of worldwide fundamentalisms that bore "striking similarities" to American fundamentalism.

Professor Ernest R. Sandeen's *The Roots of Fundamentalism: British and American Millenarianism, 1800–1930* (1970) had appeared a decade earlier and prepared the way for this development. Sandeen caused a stir among historians by proposing that American fundamentalism was a doctrinally innovative moment having its center in the Northeast of the United States. This interpretation countered a long-standing portrayal of fundamentalists as Southern agrarian anti-intellectuals.

Sandeen argued that in their coauthored article "Inspiration" (1881), Princeton Seminary theologians B. B. Warfield and A. A. Hodge created the doctrine of biblical inerrancy in the original autographs as a way to escape the negative import of higher criticism. Sandeen claimed that the doctrine had existed in neither Europe nor the United States before the 1880s. For Sandeen, the doctrine of biblical inerrancy in the original autographs became a defining doctrine of fundamentalism.

If Sandeen's interpretation is valid, fundamentalists were badly mistaken in thinking that biblical inerrancy was a Scripture-based doctrine and represented a central tradition of what Christian churches in the past had affirmed about biblical authority. These fundamentalists would have been ironically upholding a "fundamental" that dated from the late nineteenth century, not a true "fundamental" of the Christian churches throughout their history.

Ten years later, in *Fundamentalism and American Culture: The Shaping of the Twentieth Century, 1870–1925*, Professor George Marsden modified and amplified Sandeen's argument. Whereas Professor Sandeen had singled out millennialism as a principal influence shaping fundamentalist thought, Professor Marsden pointed to other roots, such as revivalism and sentiments of anguish that conservative Protestants experienced as strangers in their own land—a land that had become more religiously pluralistic and secular. In his chapter titled "The Princetonians and the

Truth," Marsden claimed that the impact of "common-sense realism" and Baconianism upon the Princetonian theologians had helped forge their static views of truth that informed their hermeneutics and innovative doctrine of biblical inerrancy: Scripture is accurate not only regarding salvation truths and ethics but even in small details regarding history and science.

A New Definition of Fundamentalism

Professor Marsden defined fundamentalism as "militantly antimodernist evangelicalism," that is, a "loose, diverse and changing federation of co-belligerents united by their fierce opposition to modernist attempts to bring Christianity into line with modern thought." Like Professor Sandeen, he indicated that the doctrine the Bible was inerrant in every detail was a "newly defined dogma" of militant fundamentalists.

Linking American Fundamentalism and Islamic Militant Fundamentalism

Professor Marsden went further and claimed that some "striking" similarities existed between American fundamentalism and Muslims' militancy and views of an infallible Koran: "Muslim fundamentalism, for example, resembles American Protestant fundamentalism in a number of striking ways. In view of its militant opposition to much of modern culture, it seems appropriate to borrow the American term to describe this Islamic phenomenon."[11]

Richard Reardon's research indicates that precedents for use of the expression "Muslim fundamentalism" did exist. As far back as 1961, an article in the *Journal of Religion and Politics in Pakistan* referenced the expression "Islamic fundamentalism." And in a 1979 article in the *Christian Century,* Bryan L. Haines protested against the use of an expression like "Islamic fundamentalist" in reference to the Ayatollah Ruhollah Khomeini. He warned that such a reference would appeal to "American stereotypes."

Nonetheless, prominent scholars joined by the media continued to make this linkage. In a pivotal 1980 *Saturday Review* article, "Fundamentalism Reborn: Faith and Fanaticism," Professor Marty E. Marty, a well-respected commentator on American religion, juxtaposed American fundamentalism and the Muslim faith. Professor Marty attributed the use of the expression *fundamentalism* to the reflections of the American press about Iran: "To get the phenomenon into focus, the media and the nation settled on a term fundamentalism. . . . Soon fundamentalism became a buzz word." According to Professor Marty, none of the groups tagged by the press as *fundamentalists* liked what was happening:

> Similarly, American Protestant fundamentalists resent being pushed into the same camp with Moslems, whom they regard as infidels. For their part, Islamic scholars protest that to borrow a term from the American experience—fundamentalism . . . and apply it to Moslems half a world away is a sign of imperialism, as if America had to provide a model for every movement, even those in other nations. Now such disclaimers have some justification. Not everyone labeled a fundamentalist is one, nor does only one kind of fundamentalism exist.[12]

But even with these reservations, Professor Marty argued that world fundamentalisms did in fact exist, exhibiting distinguishing traits of militancy and meanness. In the United States a pluralist democracy and an affluent society served as forces holding back fundamentalists from forming armies.

Professors Marty and Scott Appleby gave the world-fundamentalisms approach even greater authority by launching a massive five-year work called The Fundamentalism Project. Notable scholars compared fundamentalist religious groups from around the world that were supposed to share five traits. The first four were identified as (1) steadfast religious belief; (2) strict adherence to a moral code; (3) the practice of traditional pieties; and (4) the selective retrieval of fundamentals from a sacred text.

The fifth trait, however, was in one sense the most important because it differentiated fundamentalists from "conservatives, traditionalists, and orthodox believers." Professors Marty and Appleby proposed that "when perceiving cherished traditions, values, and ways of life to be under attack, they [fundamentalists] engage in [5] counterattack." They believed that when agitated by fear, fundamentalists strike out against their foes in defense of an imagined past when "cherished fundamentals" of their faith were allegedly pure and perfect.

In an article on fundamentalism for an encyclopedia, Professor Appleby discussed not only the selective use of modernity by fundamentalists but their selected use of the past to bolster their cause. Ostensibly relying on the interpretations of Professor Sandeen and Marsden, Appleby claimed that American fundamentalists upheld the doctrine of biblical inerrancy, which he claimed was something of their own creation and "a strategic development occasioned by a very modern problem." In other words, American fundamentalists defended selectively as an essential fundamental of the faith a doctrine that was, in reality, an innovation of the late nineteenth century.

With the prestige of distinguished commentators supporting a linkage of American fundamentalism with worldwide fundamentalisms, little wonder members of the press, editors of encyclopedias, and other gatekeepers of the culture adopted the expression *fundamentalists* to allude to members of militant religious groups worldwide.

Problems in Linking American and Islamic Fundamentalists

Given how common this usage of the expression has become in our language today, any attempt to uncouple the linkage might be thought an effort in futility. Nonetheless, scholars and members of the media would be well served to engage in some kind of reassessment out of a sense of fair play and generosity to American fundamentalists.

Reasons abound that such a reassessment is in order. First, it appears that the linkage hypothesis presumes that American fundamentalism, the alleged original standard for defining fundamentalism, has remained a static religious and social entity displaying the same traits through its history. We have seen, however, this simply is not so. Defining who a "true fundamentalist" is, even in fundamentalist circles, often depends upon the a priori beliefs of the beholder. Making one manifestation of "fundamentalism" normative for the movement is problematic at best.

Second, although a number of "fundamentalist extremists" have existed in the history of fundamentalism, resorting to personal verbal attacks—including spewing out racist and vitriolic rhetoric and at times exhibiting mean and violent behavior—they do not represent the basic thrust of this loosely federated movement. After all, the vast majority of fundamentalists of various backgrounds take the Bible very seriously. They uphold the teaching of Christ that we are to love God with all our heart, soul, and mind and our neighbors as ourselves. And many do.

This overall "loving of our neighbors" gestalt of American fundamentalism differs markedly from the gestalt of any religious ideology that encourages militants to kill in the name of their god. Many self-designated American fundamentalists have an enviable record of self-sacrifice, love, generosity, and kindness that is unfairly ignored if they are summarily linked with such religious militants. For example, in *The Smell of Sawdust: What Evangelicals Can Learn from Their Fundamentalist Heritage* (Zondervan, 2000), Richard Mouw, the president of Fuller Theological Seminary, reminds us of the very good things we can appreciate in the fundamentalist heritage from which he and many of us have come.

Third, a number of the working premises of The Fundamentalism Project are questionable. Peter Berger, one of the world's leading religious sociologists, observed that after the first volume arising from The Fundamentalism Project (entitled *Fundamentalisms Comprehended*) arrived on his desk, he recognized it as a "book weapon—the kind that could do serious injury." He proposed two reasons why the MacArthur Foundation spent millions of dollars to support this international study of religious fundamentalists: (1) "The MacArthur Foundation is a very progressive outfit, it understands fundamentalists to be anti-progressive; the Project, then, was a matter of knowing one's enemies"; (2) the project was intended to explain to elite academics the unknown world of resurgent religious groups that, by their very existence, falsified the secularization hypothesis many of the same academics had embraced.[13]

Berger's hard hitting assertion that the first volume of The Fundamentalism Project was a "weapon" should give us pause about the study's purposes and objectivity, not that we should neglect any of its impressive insights regarding other world religions.

Fourth, it is by no means clear that fundamentalists selectively espoused an imagined doctrine from the Christian past in upholding the doctrine of biblical inerrancy. A growing number of scholars have challenged the interpretation that A. A. Hodge and B. B.Warfield were the originators of the doctrine of biblical inerrancy in 1881. Clinton Ohlers' research indicates that between 1880–1900 the vast majority of theologians and pastors who defended the "errancy" of Holy Scripture acknowledged they were abandoning the old Protestant doctrine of biblical infallibility to do so. They did not perceive the "Inspiration" article of B. B. Warfield and A.A. Hodge as departing from what Protestants had earlier affirmed. Moreover, Paul Kjoss Helseth's careful research has demonstrated that the Princetonians' interaction with "common-sense realism" and Baconianism did not play the determinative role in shaping their belief in biblical inerrancy that a number of scholars have postulated.

For that matter, many Christians, whether Protestant or Roman Catholic, believed that the Bible was infallible for matters of faith and practice and history and science (the equivalent of the inerrancy position) long before the 1880s. In *Biblical Higher Criticism and the Defense of Infallibilism in 19th Century Britain* (1987), Nigel Cameron demonstrates that large segments of the English public upheld this belief in the first half of the nineteenth century. The English were not alone in the West. As far back as 1518 the Roman Catholic Johannes Eck in a debate with Erasmus claimed that all Christians believed that the Bible was without error after Erasmus had indicated that Matthew, due to a slip in memory, had made a mistake in Matthew 2:6. Eck would not accept the contention that there was even a small error in Scripture. "Listen, dear Erasmus: do you suppose any Christian will patiently endure to be told that the evangelists in their Gospels made mistakes? If the authority of Holy Scripture at this point is shaky, can any other passage be free from the suspicion of error?"[14]

Earlier still, Augustine upheld the Bible's infallibility: "For it seems to me that most disastrous consequences must follow upon our believing that anything false is found in the sacred books."[15] Elsewhere he wrote: "I have learned to yield this respect and honor only to the canonical books of Scripture: of these alone do I most firmly believe that the authors were completely free from error."[16] Regarding supposed errors in Scripture, Augustine gave this advice: "If we are perplexed by an apparent contradiction in Scripture, it is not allowable to say, The author of this book is mistaken; but either the manuscript is faulty, or the translation is wrong, or you have not understood."

Fifth, it's highly questionable to label American fundamentalism of the 1920s as a movement of doctrinal innovation that departed from essential teachings of earlier Christian churches. Even some of the harshest critics agreed with the fundamentalists' claims that they were seeking to uphold the fundamentals of the faith. For example, in 1926, John H. Dietrich, a Unitarian, wrote in the *Humanist Pulpit,* "Fundamentalism is simply a forceful reaffirmation of Christian faith and authority. The name is very suggestive, for it means that they have taken as a basis for their religion what has been considered fundamental to Christianity. So there is nothing new about Fundamentalism—it is merely orthodox Christianity."[17]

Sixth, a number of moderate Muslim commentators dislike the application of the expression *fundamentalist* to religious extremists in their midst. This usage gives the impression that the beliefs of the extremists actually represent the fundamentals of the Muslim faith, when in fact they do not.

These six points alone argue for a careful rethinking of the linkage between religious extremists who are willing to kill for their god and American fundamentalists. The linkage should in fact be uncoupled.

FUNDAMENTALISM AND THE MARK OF JESUS

If non-Christians identify the word *fundamentalist* with anyone who proposes that Jesus Christ is the way, the truth, and the life, then for them we are all fundamentalists, whether we call ourselves evangelicals, fundamentalists, or something else. Regardless of what we are called, we should be glad and honored to say that Jesus is the only way to God.

Unfortunately, many non-Christians who use the word *fundamentalist* in this fashion often load it with negative connotations like mean-spirited, intolerant, coercive, and prone to violence. By pigeonholing believers in this way, it is difficult for non-Christians to see the mark of Jesus upon us.

What to do? We could simply ignore the problem. But then the misrepresentations we have discussed may take on an even greater shelf life in our popular culture. Another approach would be for cultural apologists to step forward to craft careful studies that are winsome, graceful, and certainly nonbelligerent, in which various meanings of the word *fundamentalist* are unpacked for a general public. We cannot blame the media and others for their assumptions about fundamentalists if they do not have access to resources (including *human* resources) explaining why linking American fundamentalism to religious extremists is unfair and academically untenable.

Literature could be made available to reiterate the point that the vast majority of Christians who call themselves fundamentalists or evangelicals or charismatics or confessional Christians sincerely believe in the rights of conscience for atheists, agnostics, and followers of other world religions. No authentic contradiction exists between a Christian affirming that Jesus Christ is the way, the truth, and the life and defending the religious rights of those who do not share that conviction. Christians have rich biblical and historical resources from which to draw in making this case. Unfortunately, many non-Christians are unaware of believers' commitment to the rights of conscience for others.

If members of an adult Sunday school class were already fearful of fundamentalists in the mid-1980s, we should make every effort to let the larger public know today that we believe fully in the rights of others to hold their own beliefs. But words must be joined with actions. We cannot be mean-spirited. We must bear the mark of the Christian (showing love to our neighbors) in how we interact with our brothers and sisters in Christ and in how we treat non-Christians with genuine respect and dignity, esteeming their worth.

We may want to ponder the old Puritan prayer, a portion of which reads: "Help me to be always devoted, confident, obedient, resigned, childlike in my trust of thee, to love thee with soul, body, mind, strength, to love my fellow-man as I love myself, to be saved from unregenerate temper, hard thoughts, slanderous words, meanness, unkind manners, to master my tongue and keep the door of my lips. Fill me with grace daily, that my life be a fountain of sweet water."[18]

If we view ourselves as fundamentalists, we should be careful not to indulge in unseemly rhetoric when we speak of evangelicals and others who do not share all of our convictions about the nature of biblical separation. We may guard and advocate our views without speaking ill of others. If we view ourselves as confessional Christians, upholding particular creeds like the Westminster Confession, we might embrace J. Gresham Machen's generous attitude toward other believers who did not share fully his Reformed commitments. Likewise, if we view ourselves as evangelicals, we may seek to refrain from engaging in any form of "put-down" rhetoric in talking about fundamentalists, confessional Christians, Pentecostals, and others. Nor should we play to the galleries of critics by calling fellow Christians fundamentalists if we are using the term in a pejorative way.

Often our harsh words about others flow from hearts steeped in spiritual pride. We may have a critical spirit, making criticism of others one of our common practices. But this is not the biblical way. In Ephesians 4:1–3, Paul tells us to walk worthy of the vocation with which we are called and "be completely humble and gentle; be patient, bearing with one another in love. Make every effort to keep the unity of the Spirit through the bond of peace." This attitude does not mean that we believe doctrine is unimportant or that we and other people cannot be mistaken. Right doctrine is critically important. Nonetheless, Paul indicates that we are to speak the truth in love in seeking to see the church built up whose head is Christ (Ephesians 4:15).

If we live in this way, non-Christians may be able to see the mark of Jesus upon us as we seek to uphold the fundamentals of the faith that speak of our wonderful Master and Savior, Jesus Christ.

But What About

People of
Other Religions?

September the eleventh. So momentous were the events
that happened on this date that it is no longer necessary to add the year,
2001. On that date, Muslim terrorists, acting in the name of God, and
citing sacred texts, launched a surprise attack on the United States of
America. September 11 was a rude awakening for many who had assumed
that such an event could not happen here. Indeed, who could have pre-
dicted that such a small group of religious zealots could strike such a blow
against the strongest nation in the world?

Before the shock had worn off, Christians had begun to reflect on the
religious meaning of this historic event. Some church leaders speculated
that the attacks of September 11 were God's judgment against America
for permitting such horrible practices as abortion on demand to go
unchecked, for shoving God and prayer out of the public school system,
and so forth. Christians also faced anew the issue of religious pluralism:

Many competing religious communities with contradictory belief systems now vie for allegiance here in America as well as in places far away. How are Christians to respond to the fact that there are so many "alien gods on American turf," as one writer has put it?

One of the most common objections against accepting the Christian faith in today's world stems from the fact that the gospel of Christ has been presented historically as the only authentic pathway to eternal life. But is this really true? Is Jesus Christ the only Savior, or merely one savior among many? How Christians respond to this question—one that is often sincerely asked by honest seekers after the truth—will determine to a great extent whether our witness for Christ will be seen as credible in a world that more than ever needs to know the good news about God's gift of salvation. Our strategy in this chapter is, first, to look at two theological dead ends in dealing with the issue of religious pluralism; then to examine two case studies from the past (from the lives of the apostle Paul and the missionary William Carey), both of which provide important lessons for us today. Finally, we will list several strategic initiatives about how to share an uncompromised Gospel message in the spirit and love of Christ.

TWO MISTAKES

Since September 11, there have been two basic responses to Christian-Muslim relations, and to the wider issue of competing religious truth claims. Both are fundamentally unhelpful to believers who seek to engage the question, "What about people of other religions?" The first response is characterized by harsh, unmitigated, frequently angry denunciation. The second approach follows the pathway of open, undiscerning and usually uncritical pluralism. As we look at each of these strategies, it becomes clear that Christians who want to share God's love and grace with persons from other faith traditions should avoid both of these theological byways.

The Rhetoric of Denunciation

The rhetoric of denunciation is often fueled by fear and misunderstanding. This is particularly true in the case of Islam. When we hear of Christians being persecuted and put to death because of their faith in Christ in Muslim lands, and when we consider that the militant Muslims who committed the atrocities of September 11 appealed to religious values and sacred writings to justify their violent acts, it is easy to think that all Muslims are terrorists, or at least terrorist sympathizers. A harsh verdict against Islam in general is further fueled by the fact that most of what we know about Islam—and this is true of other religions as well—is based on sketchy, incomplete information. For example, most Americans tend to think that most Muslims live in the Middle East. This is doubtless because the Israeli-Palestinian conflict, the war in Iraq, and other conflicts in the volatile Middle East are featured night after night on the evening news. But, in fact, only 15 percent of the world's Muslims live in the Middle East. The largest Muslim country today is Indonesia, a country far removed, politically and culturally as well as geographically, from the Arab world.

One of the important facts about contemporary culture is the increasingly non-geographic identification of world religious communities. New York City has far more Jews than Tel Aviv or Jerusalem. Leicester, a city in the English Midlands, from which the Baptist missionary William Carey went to India, is now filled with Sikh temples. France, traditionally a Roman Catholic country, has a significant and growing Muslim minority. Current trends in immigration, globalization, and information technology all point to a further erosion of traditional boundaries.

There are several reasons why Christians should be cautious in issuing condemnatory verdicts—"evangelical fatwas" we might call them—against the followers of non-Christian religions. Most important, perhaps, is that this approach does not match the strategy of Jesus Himself. "For God did not send his Son into the world to condemn the world, but to save the world through him" (John 3:17). Now it is certainly true that the entire world outside of Christ does stand under the wrath and judgment of God; yet it is only in the light of Christ, especially in the light of God's love, which sent Jesus to the cross, that lost human beings can begin to grasp the extent and depth of their alienation from God. Our task is to approach the lost and unevangelized not with a wagging finger but with a loving heart.

We evangelicals love to quote the Great Commission in the words of Jesus found in the closing verses of Matthew's gospel. We sometimes forget that there is another version of the Great Commission found in the gospel of John. "As my Father hath sent me," Jesus said to His disciples, "even so send I you" (John 20:21 KJV). Those little connecting words "as . . . even so" established the parameters within which all of our efforts to reach out to others in Jesus' name should take place. In other words, there is a direct connection between what we say in our Christian witness and how we say it, just as there is a direct correlation between the *words* of our message and our daily *walk* before a watching world. First Peter 3:15 tells us to "always be prepared to give an answer to everyone who asks you to give the reason for the hope that you have." But this same verse also tells us how this important task is to be done, namely, "with gentleness and respect."

A second reason why our denouncing persons of other religious traditions will not lead many of them to trust in Jesus is that such words invariably come across as marked by meanness and an air of superiority rather than by gratitude and humility. We must beware of engaging in a kind of "my-God's-better-than-your-God" religious cheerleading contest lest we fall into the trap of the Pharisee who made a great show of external piety—"I thank Thee, God, that I am not as this man is"—but went home puffed with pride and unjustified in the Lord's sight. This kind of braggadocio usually has very little to do with the Gospel itself. More often than not, it masks our promotion of a particular culture or political program. Lesslie Newbigin, a twentieth-century missionary to India, remarked that at the very heart of the biblical vision "is not an imperial power but the slain Lamb."[1]

There is still another reason that harsh condemnation is not the best way to approach this issue. Sometimes our statements, spoken from the relative ease and safety of our position here at home, may reverberate throughout the world in ways that have dire consequences for our fellow believers and Christian missionaries who serve in difficult and dangerous places. Following September 11, and some of the highly publicized remarks of Christian leaders in the West about Islam as a wicked, heinous religion, a group of evangelical missionaries working in predominately Muslim countries issued an open letter calling for sensitivity among those who speak out on this issue back home.

> Comments by Christians in the West about Islam and Muhammad can and do receive much attention in our cities and communities on local radio, television, and print sources. These types of comments . . . can further the already heightened animosity toward Christians, more so toward evangelicals. We have found it more beneficial with our Muslim friends to concentrate on sharing Christ in love and concentrating on the message of the Gospel, instead of speaking in a degrading manner about their religion or prophet.[2]

In bearing faithful witness to the gospel of Christ in a world of religious diversity, Christians should always remember the three questions asked by Paul in 1 Corinthians 4:7. First, who has made us any different than anyone else? Second, what do we have that we did not receive? The only honest answer anyone can give to this question is "Nothing, nothing at all." And, third, if indeed we have received all that we have as a gift, why on earth should we boast and brag as though it were ours by right? Evangelism, D. T. Niles famously remarked, is one beggar telling another beggar where to find a piece of bread. Authentic Christian witness, the kind characterized by the mark of Jesus, is always free of proud illusions.

The Pitfall of Uncritical Pluralism

If the attitude of harsh condemnation is often found among theologically conservative Christians, the opposite error, uncritical pluralism, is a hallmark of a theologically liberal approach to faith. Like the first alternative we have discussed, this view is also motivated by fear, but fear of a different sort. Deeply held religious convictions, it is said, are the source of much of the world's conflict and violence today. Thus we must somehow transcend theological differences and divergent belief systems in order to achieve a lasting harmony among the peoples of the world.

This view seems to be gaining ground in our current postmodern culture, but it is really nothing new. In 1932 seven mainline American Protestant denominations convened a committee which published a report in a book entitled *Living Religions and a World Faith*. This report declared that the task of the evangelist and missionary "is to see the best in other religions, to help the adherents of those religions to discover, or to rediscover, all that is best in their own traditions. . . . The aim should not be *conversion*. The ultimate aim . . . is the emergence of the various religions out of their isolation into a world fellowship in which each will find its appropriate place."[3] The principal author of this report was William Ernest Hocking, a Congregationalist lay leader who also taught philosophy at Harvard University. What the world needs, Hocking said, is a universal generic religion, one not marked by "the staleness of ancient subjectivities." "God is in the world," he said, "but Buddha, Jesus, Muhammad are in their little private closets and we should thank them but never return to them."

The denominations that sponsored this report have largely given up on the task of recruiting and sending missionaries to share the message of Christ with those who have never heard of Him. When they speak of "mission" at all, it is defined in terms of political liberation, social programs, ecological concerns, feminism, and the like. This development represents a great reversal for these denominations that were once at the forefront of the great advance in missions history associated with the heroic labors of Adoniram and Anne Judson, David Livingstone, Hudson Taylor, and many others.

What we have called uncritical pluralism is not so much one particular theory of religion as it is an attitude that denies the exclusive truth claims of any distinctive faith tradition. One version of this approach is syncretism, an effort to amalgamate divergent religions into one single homogenized whole. This approach can be expressed in beautiful poetic language that is alluringly seductive. Thomas Cahill, writing in the introduction to a beautiful picture book entitled *Holy Lands: One Place, Three Faiths,* presents a vision of Judaism, Christianity, and Islam forming a single, undifferentiated faith, in which "though they call me by different names, / I have one name common to all, / For Peace is the name of the Lord."[4]

Given the long history of bloodshed and rancor among these three monotheistic religious traditions, what could possibly be wrong with such a beautiful vision? Two things. Simply put, it's both dishonest and disrespectful. Dishonest because it ignores the clear irreducible differences, differences about ultimate realities, that separate these three "Abrahamic religions," this despite the shared history and significant similarities they do have in common. Disrespectful because it is based on a paternalistic view of religious unity not shared by devout believers of any one of these traditions. Instead, those on the outside have imposed a unity based on an extraneous agenda.

As we have said throughout this book, Christians who would bear the mark of Jesus must ever seek to speak the truth in love. But speak the truth we must! Near the end of her life, Simone Weil, who came to the Christian faith after a long and torturous pilgrimage, said of this necessity, "Christ likes us to prefer truth to him because, before being Christ, he is Truth. If one turns aside from him to go toward the truth, one will not go far before falling into his arms."[5]

WITH PAUL IN ATHENS

Before we turn to some practical suggestions for reaching out in love with the message of Christ to persons who belong to non-Christian religions, we want to look briefly at two famous examples of how this was done in the past. The first example comes from the Bible. It is the account of Paul's encounter with the Athenians on Mars Hill, as recorded in Acts 17.

A Burden Motivated by Love

Paul's brief missionary sojourn in Athens has a great deal to teach us about our approach to followers of other religions. His burden for the Athenians is evident from the fact that he was "greatly distressed" (verse 16) when he observed the idolatry on display everywhere there. The Greek word for "distressed" is *paroxyn,* sometimes translated "irritated" (Moffatt) or "exasperated" (New English Bible) or even "deeply troubled" (New Living Translation). The Greek word has medical connotations associated with seizures and epileptic fits. It further connotes a state of being not only distressed and upset but also angry (as in 1 Corinthians 13:5, where we are told that love is not "easily angered"). What was Paul mad about as he walked through the streets of Athens? Why is it that "his spirit was stirred in him" by what he saw (verse 16 KJV)?

Clearly, he was disturbed when he considered the utter vanity of idol worship, when he thought about the final destiny of those who were mired in a system of belief and religious practice that would one day terminate in death and judgment, a point he will later make in his sermon (verse 31). However, it is important to note that Paul's anger did not terminate on the people he saw or those with whom he talked. What motivated Paul to go to Athens in the first place? What prompted his distress and gave such an urgency to his discussions? The answer is obvious from his life and writings: the love of God. "For Christ's love compels us. . . . we are therefore Christ's ambassadors, as though God were making his appeal through us. We implore you on Christ's behalf: Be reconciled to God" (2 Corinthians 5:14, 20).

This same motivation must undergird our own Christian witness today. As we encounter those who follow non-Christian systems of worship and practice, we cannot be content with idle curiosity, nor must we approach these persons with our evangelical guns "loaded for bear." We come in love, bearing witness to the truth of the Gospel in a way that commends the urgent word we have been sent to proclaim.

Why do we do this? Because the Gospel itself is inherently commendable, it "deserves full acceptance" (1 Timothy 1:15). Because this is true, then, we must never forget that we follow not the Christ of the clenched fist but rather the Messiah who died with outstretched arms.

A Message Sensitive to the Audience

While in Athens Paul spoke with different types of people and used a strategy of witness appropriate to each group. Following his normal pattern, he first went to the synagogue where he "reasoned" with the Jews and God-fearing Greek seekers who were present there. In that setting Paul no doubt appealed to the work of God and the history of Israel as recorded in the Old Testament Scriptures. However, when he encountered the Athenian philosophers, he took a very different approach. He did not change the content of the message he proclaimed, but he contextualized his witness in a way that was appropriate to the worldview and level of understanding of those he encountered. In both cases, he ended at the same place, but he used varying apologetic strategies to get there!

Let's look at five major emphases in Paul's address to the stoic and epicurean philosophers of Athens.

A Message on the Human Situation

Paul began with what he saw as he walked through the streets of Athens. "Men of Athens! I see that in every way you are very religious. For as I walked around and observed your objects of worship, I even found an altar with this inscription: TO AN UNKNOWN GOD" (Acts 17:22–23). Paul then promised that he would reveal to them the identity of this unknown deity after whom they were blindly groping in the dark.

In other words, Paul began where the people of Athens were, and he found a point of contact in their worship of the unknown God. Significantly, he did not go in with guns blazing, demanding that all of the altars to the false gods in Athens be overturned and the idols they worshiped be smashed to pieces. In other places, Paul took a more confrontational approach. For example, in Ephesus he openly declared that "man-made gods are no gods at all" (Acts 19:26). This led to a riot among the silversmiths of that city who feared, with some reason no doubt, that their business was in jeopardy. In Athens, Paul was dealing with a different constituency, and he took a different approach.

At the same time, Paul did not merely endorse the pattern of worship he observed in Athens, however sincere and devout it may have been. He rather nudged the Athenians to acknowledge the limitation and inadequacy to which their own religious practice testified. By beginning with the human situation, by starting with the questions provoked by the restlessness and mystery that confronts human beings everywhere, Paul gained access to enter into a more constructive conversation and dialogue.

What gave Paul the right to take this approach? He had read the Athenian culture as well as his Bible (which for him, of course, was the Old Testament), and he had learned how to present the Gospel in a contextually appropriate manner. He also knew that, ultimately, the True Evangelist is the Holy Spirit. He alone can open the hearts and minds of those to whom we bear witness. In starting with the human condition though, we encourage further probings, deeper soundings, more careful investigations, and wider readings.

A Message on Creation

Having unmasked the pretensions of Athenian religion, as it were, Paul then moved to declare the primal fact about God: He is the Creator of everyone and everything everywhere. This God is sovereign and independent of the kind of needs and desires that marked the identity of the deities who dwelled "in temples built by hands."

It is important to note that this was a countercultural doctrine of creation. The Greek philosophers, following Plato, all believed that matter was eternal, and that creation was merely the reshaping of a primordial, preexistent kind of "stuff" by some divine being who was actually more of a craftsman than a creator. In contrast, Paul declared that the true God had made the world and everything in it out of nothing, by an act of His will and for His own purposes. If this reading of reality is right, then it means that we have a much bigger God than the Greek pagan religion allowed for. This point allowed Paul to move on to his next major emphasis.

A Message on Providence and History

Having established that God is the Creator of all that is, Paul next described how this same God has been active in human history all along, guiding it toward its appointed end through His providential care. When the Bible teaches that God created the world, this is more than a statement about God's omnipotence. In other words, creation means more than merely affirming that in the beginning God said "poof" and, with that pronouncement, the cosmos popped into being. No, to claim, as Paul does here, that God is the creator of all that is implies that God has been active in human history all along. God has not abandoned the world, nor humankind to their own devices. While we may not even realize it, and while we may sometimes have difficulty explaining precisely how this is worked out in every particular event, we know that God is constantly intervening in human history, even to the point of determining "the times set for [the nations] and the exact places where they should live" (verse 26).

History, in other words, is purpose-driven. History is going somewhere: It, no less than the created order itself, moves in a trajectory of divine design, even as the created order does. This is a perspective that Christianity shares in common with Judaism and Islam, but not with Buddhism, Hinduism, and other religions of the East.

A Message on Accountability

Paul then extended his argument by declaring that the God of creation and history is also the God of final judgment. Even though the Athenians claimed to worship an "unknown God," such ignorance does not exempt them from accountability before the bar of divine justice, Paul argued. Thus Paul continued his argument from general revelation: God has not left Himself without a witness in the cosmos He has designed and made, nor in the human conscience. Paul told his listeners that "we live and move and have our being" (verse 28) in the Creator-God. He did not hesitate to back up this point by quoting from the pagan poets who were well known to the educated men of Athens.

As we enter discussions with non-Christian religious people today, we too can follow Paul's strategy of identifying and holding up God's truth wherever we may find it. Samuel Zwemer, the great Presbyterian missionary to the Muslims, once declared that we can best help our Muslim friends answer the question, "What think ye of Christ?" and thus lead them to higher truth, by acknowledging all of the truth that they possess.

A Message on Christology

Having begun with the human situation, then having affirmed creation, God's providential guidance of history, and the final accountability all humans will face at the judgment, Paul next revealed the true identity of the "unknown God" to the Athenians. "For [God] has set a day when he will judge the world with justice by the man he has appointed. He has given proof of this to all men by raising him from the dead" (verse 31). While we do not know everything Paul said in this message, we can be sure that he did not bypass the great facts of the incarnation and the atonement as he preached "the good news about Jesus and the resurrection" (verse 18).

The burden of Paul's message was a refusal to acquiesce to the relativism and pluralism of the religious culture of his day. The one thing he could not do was to place Jesus on an equal par with other deities. He could not construct a new altar to Jesus and place it alongside the countless others he had seen in Athens. To epicureanism with its pessimism and to stoicism with its pantheism, Paul declared that life is not just a meaningless struggle "full of sound and fury, signifying nothing" (as Shakespeare would write more than a millennium later). God has made us all in His image, he said, and one day we will have a rendezvous in eternity with Him. There is a man in heaven, even Jesus, who stands forever at the borders of two worlds. He is the Alpha and the Omega, the beginning and the end, the first and the last. So repent, Paul said, and embrace the forgiveness that is offered through Jesus Christ. Paul ended his message by an invitation: an invitation to destiny, a destiny fit for eternity.

A Mixed Response

What was the response to Paul's distinctive approach to the worshipers of other gods in Athens? The response was mixed. Some rejected what he said outright, with sarcasm and a sneer. Others were intellectually curious and wanted to hear more about Jesus and His resurrection from the dead. But there were also a few who believed. We know two of their names, Dionysius and Damaris. Dionysius was a member of the council on Mars Hill to whom Paul had spoken. Damaris was a woman of the city.

Some have considered Paul's mission to Athens a dismal failure because only a few were converted to Christ on that occasion. However, Paul's words in Athens have continued to echo down the centuries of church history. Many others have become believers in Jesus by following the footsteps of the apostle to the Athenians.

WITH CAREY IN INDIA

On June 13, 1793, William Carey, his wife, Dorothy, and their four children, including a nursing infant, sailed from England on a Danish ship headed for India. Carey remained in India until his death in 1834, forty-one years of devoted service and Gospel witness among persons who knew nothing of Christ and the story of His love revealed in the Scriptures. Today Carey is revered as the "father of modern missions" by devout Christians of all denominations. But he is also recognized and honored by the people of India, the vast majority of whom are not Christians at all, because of the way in which he carried out his evangelistic labors while contributing in a formative way to many aspects of Indian life including education, journalism, agriculture, and the development of human rights for all persons. Let's look at three aspects of Carey's amazing mission to India.

An Uncompromised Gospel

First, Carey preached an uncompromised Gospel in a culture of pluralism. Carey never wavered in presenting Jesus Christ as the unique Son of God and the sole and sufficient Savior for all persons everywhere. Had Carey accepted the premise of some contemporary missiological thinking, he would never have gone to India in the first place or, had he done so, he would have embraced there the indigenous Hindu belief that all religions are equally valid paths to the one unknowable god. In his many conversations and encounters with Hindus and Muslims, Carey always insisted that Jesus Christ is "the *only medium* through which man can approach God" (emphasis added). On one occasion he declared that there were two nonnegotiable teachings of New Testament Christianity: "That God views all sin as so abominable that the death of Jesus Christ alone can expiate its guilt; and that the human heart is so corrupt that it must be renewed by the Divine Spirit before a man can enter heaven . . . without these two dogmas, what is the Gospel?"[6]

Like Paul in Athens, Carey had a mixed reception in India. His emphasis on the finality of Jesus Christ, and the need for every person to repent and embrace the Gospel, flew in the face of the prevailing syncretism he saw on display all around him as he walked through the busy streets of Calcutta. "Go where you will," he said, "and you are sure to see something of an idolatrous kind: flowers, trees, or little temples by the wayside." Yet, like Paul before him, he saw the world through the eyes of the Savior's love, and this compelled him to continue to share the good news of salvation through Jesus Christ with the people of India. On one occasion, he said:

> I feel something of what Paul felt when he beheld Athens, and "his spirit
> was stirred within him." I see one of the finest countries in the world,
> full of industrious inhabitants; yet three-fifths of it are an uncultivated

jungle, abandoned to wild beasts and serpents. If the Gospel flourishes here, "the wilderness will in every respect become a fruitful field."[7]

Carey faced many difficulties. For seven years he continued to work—translating the Scriptures, preaching in the marketplaces, learning the language and culture of those around him—before making a single convert to the Christian faith. On December 28, 1800, the little missionary community Carey had established at Serampore went to the riverside for the baptism of Krishna Pal, a Hindu carpenter who had come to trust in Christ through attending the Bible studies at the mission house. Carey rejoiced that God had permitted him to "desecrate the Ganges" by baptizing the first Hindu believer. Krishna Pal soon became an evangelist himself. He declared: "Going forth, I will proclaim the love of Christ with rejoicing. To sinners I will say this word: Here sinner, brother! Without Christ there is no help. Christ, the world to save, gave his own soul! Such compassion, where shall we get?"[8]

The Gospel Set in Context

Second, Carey was a pioneer in contextualizing the Gospel in a cross-cultural setting. Contextualization refers to the need to communicate the Gospel in such a way that it speaks to the total context of the people to whom it is addressed. Carey was willing to experiment with new methods and to use untried approaches in reaching for Christ the people to whom he had been sent. The establishment of indigenous churches and the training of native pastors were two key elements in his plan for permeating India with the Gospel. Realizing that male missionaries would have limited access to female hearers in the Hindu and Muslim cultures, he encouraged the cultivation of "Bible women" who were often able to break through the gender barrier to share a positive witness to Christ. This tradition of female Christian evangelism still continues in India today.

Carey was able to make these adaptations because he had gone to India not merely to convert the people there from one "religion" to another, much less to import an alien culture or civilization, but rather to proclaim the life-changing, culture-transforming message of salvation through repentance and faith in Jesus Christ. He did not aim to eradicate the positive values of Indian culture. He had great respect for the antiquity and beauty of the cultural legacy he encountered. Indeed, his translations and critical editions of the ancient Hindu classics contributed to what has been called an "Indian Renaissance." At the same time, he was quite sure that devotion to these writings and the religion they had spawned could never lead to eternal life, any more than being born in England or America automatically made one a Christian.

Carey's ability to contextualize the Gospel without compromising the essentials of Christian doctrine provides a balanced model as we seek to do the same thing in our own age of social upheaval and cultural dissolution.

A Genuine Concern for People

And, finally, Carey backed up his direct evangelistic appeals with a genuine concern for the physical and social as well as the spiritual needs of his hearers. Speaking to the International Congress on World Evangelization at Lausanne in 1974, Billy Graham outlined five concepts which may be taken as hallmarks of a biblical approach to evangelism: (1) the authority of the Scriptures; (2) the lostness of human beings apart from Jesus Christ; (3) salvation in Jesus Christ alone; (4) a witness to the Gospel in word and deed; and (5) the necessity of evangelism. The fourth principle, declaring the Good News "in word and deed," points to the dual necessity of *both* declaring *and* living (i.e., including a propositional and incarnational dimension to) the mission of the church.

Carey steadfastly refused to divorce conversion from discipleship. He knew that Jesus had given food to hungry people on the same occasion that He presented Himself as the Bread of Life. He would have agreed with the statement of E. Stanley Jones, a great Methodist missionary to India in the twentieth century: A soul without a body is a ghost; a body without a soul is a corpse. The Gospel is addressed to living persons, soul and body, in all of their broken humanity and need for wholeness.

Although Carey never lost sight of the individual, he saw clearly that the Christian message also applied to the sinful social structures of his day. He vigorously opposed slavery and rejoiced when the slave trade was abolished within the British Empire shortly before his death. He urged legislation to curb the inhuman practices of *sati* (the Hindu ritual of burning widows alive) and infanticide (the tossing of newborn babies into the Ganges River as an offering to the gods). He detested the wanton destruction wrought by war and prayed for peace among the nations of the world. Carey prayed and worked to transform the structures of oppression in the light of the holistic Gospel of redemption and deliverance.

Carey's Legacy

Carey's mission to India was a catalyst for a great missionary awakening throughout the church. Carey's love for the people of India and his sensitivity to the setting and context of those among whom he lived and witnessed make him a good model for us today. In the year 2000, more than ten thousand evangelists, theologians, mission strategists, and church leaders from more than two hundred countries assembled in Amsterdam where they set forth a charter for evangelism in the twenty-first century known as "The Amsterdam Declaration." The section on religious pluralism and evangelism reflects the legacy and embodies the spirit of William Carey:

> Today's evangelist is called to proclaim the Gospel in an increasingly pluralistic world. In this global village of competing faiths and many world religions, it is important that our evangelism be marked both by faithfulness to the Good News of Christ and humility in our delivery of it. Because God's general revelation extends to all points of his creation, there may well be traces of truth, beauty and goodness in many non-Christian belief systems. But we have no warrant for regarding any of these as alternative Gospels or separate roads to salvation. The only way to know God in peace, love and joy is the reconciling death of Jesus Christ the risen Lord. As we share this message with others, we must do so with love and humility shunning all arrogance, hostility and disrespect. As we enter into dialogue with adherence of other religions, we must be courteous

and kind. But such dialogue must not be a substitute for proclamation. Yet because all persons are made in the image of God, we must advocate religious liberty and human rights for all. We pledge ourselves to treat those of other faiths with respect and faithfully and humbly to serve the nation in which God has placed us, while affirming that Christ is the one and only Savior of the world.[9]

SEVEN STRATEGIES

How can Christians exhibit the mark of Jesus as we reach out to share the love of Christ with those who belong to other religions? How can we bear a faithful witness to the Gospel without coming across as arrogant and belligerent? Here are seven strategies we recommend.

1. Seek to Understand the Person's Beliefs and Practices

We should understand the beliefs and religious practices of those we hope will give a fair hearing to the claims of Christ. It is important to avoid generalizations and to clear away misconceptions and stereotypes of non-Christian religions. This means we will have to do some serious research and study. This also means that we will need to cultivate the art of listening as well as speaking as we seek to gain a fuller understanding and an accurate analysis of other faith traditions. One of the most important of the biblical commandments is that we should not bear false witness against our neighbors. This is always important, but nowhere more so than when we are describing those beliefs and teachings that are held sacred by our neighbors who belong to other religious traditions.

2. Develop Personal Relationships

We should cultivate personal relationships with those who belong to a different religious tradition. In John 4, Jesus encountered a woman of Samaria at Jacob's well in the town of Sychar. The Samaritans followed religious traditions different from those of the Jews, who regarded them as outside orthodox faith. Later in the conversation, Jesus would delve deeply into the personal and spiritual concerns of this woman. But His point of contact with her was the simple question, "Will you give me a drink?"

Simply to recognize the common humanity of other persons can help to establish a link for further relationship and even friendship. Once a level of trust is established, we can open our hearts and our homes for further explorations and discussions.

3. Work Together

We should work together for the common good on matters of mutual concern. On many pressing issues of public policy today, Christians share with many adherents of other religions a commitment to morality, civility, and human rights. For example, the Alliance for Marriage includes Christians from both the Protestant and Catholic traditions as well as Muslims, Jews, and others who wish to preserve the legal basis of marriage between one man and one woman. We can join with many of these same persons in opposing abortion on demand, unregulated stem cell research, euthanasia, pornography, the sexual exploitation of children, and much more. As Jesus taught, God pours His common grace out indiscriminately on all persons everywhere, causing the sun to shine and the rain to fall on the just and unjust alike (cf. Matthew 5:45).

We can work with persons of goodwill from many different religious traditions to advance all that is good and tolerable in human life, all that is noble and praiseworthy in the realms of politics, culture, science, art, music, literature, etc. This does not mean that common grace and general revelation alone are sufficient to bring lost persons into a saving relationship with God. But it does provide a solid basis for co-operation and co-belligerency between Christians and followers of other religions on many issues of critical importance in society today.

4. Refrain from Ecumenical Compromise

We should avoid inappropriate services of joint worship where the distinctive truth claims of Christianity are denied or downplayed. We have no biblical warrant for engaging in the kind of easygoing inter-faith ecumenism that assumes that all persons of religious commitment are pursuing equally valid pathways to God.

If called upon to offer a prayer in an interfaith setting, do so only if you are free to pray in the name of Jesus, making clear your Christian convictions to all present. On the other hand, seek out opportunities for social interaction and mutual encouragement with those from other faith traditions. For example, a conservative Presbyterian congregation (PCA) in Atlanta, in a surprising initiative, invited the members of a neighboring mosque to share a Sunday evening potluck supper at their church. This was not a joint worship service but a time of getting ac-quainted and sharing mutual concern about their common community life. Several weeks later, the Muslim imam invited the Christian church to his mosque in a reciprocal gesture. On occasions like this, we can demonstrate the love of Christ for our neighbors while maintaining our spiritual integrity and theological convictions.

5. Avoid Speculation

One of the most hotly debated questions within the evangelical church today concerns the possibility of salvation among the unevan-gelized. What will happen to those who have never heard the message of Christ in this life? While such questions raise significant theological issues, it is important that we not give way to theological curiosity and speculation that goes beyond God's clearly revealed will in Scripture. For example, on this controversial question, it is clear that God will judge everyone on the basis of the light they have received, and that in the end His judgment will be seen by all to be perfectly righteous. "Will not the Judge of all the earth do right?" (Genesis 18:25).

On the final day of reckoning no one who has ever lived will be able to say to the Lord, "You have dealt unjustly with me." And, while God ever remains sovereign in His dealings with humankind, we have no reason to go beyond the clear teaching of Scripture which declares, "Sal-vation is found in no one else, for there is no other name under heaven given to men by which we must be saved" (Acts 4:12).

6. Be a Positive Witness

We are to share a positive witness of God's redeeming love in Jesus Christ. Christians have sometimes been drawn into debates with followers of other religions in the interest of defending the truth. There may well be a place for such debates, but, as the best Christian apologists have always known, it is possible to win an argument and lose a soul. Another approach is inter-religious dialogue, and this too can contribute to greater mutual understanding, but, at the end of the day, the Christian is under a different burden, a different obligation. "I am not ashamed of the gospel," Paul wrote to the Romans, "because it is the power of God for the salvation of everyone who believes" (Romans 1:16).

One of the best ways to present the Gospel message to persons of different religious traditions is to invite them to read the Scriptures with you. Many of them will never have read before the New Testament account of Jesus' life, death, and resurrection. The Bible, invigorated by the Holy Spirit, can break through barriers to faith in Christ that our best reasoning and persuasive arguments cannot overcome.

7. Pray

While God can work sovereignly and unilaterally to accomplish His purposes, we know that it pleases Him to use the prayers of His people to advance the cause of the Gospel. As Paul wrote to the Corinthians, "On him we have set our hope that he will continue to deliver us, as you help us by your prayers" (2 Corinthians 1:10–11). Speaking at the Keswick Convention in 1915, Samuel Zwemer offered the following prayer: "Oh God, to whom the Muslim world bows in homage five times daily, look in mercy upon its people and reveal to them thy Christ." Today there is an international network of prayer on behalf of Muslim peoples through out the world. We should be no less fervent in our prayers for those who have not yet trusted in Jesus Christ in all of the world's religious traditions.

In his faraway mission post in India, William Carey frequently felt isolated from his fellow believers back home in England, and he sometimes grew despondent. But he was greatly encouraged when he realized that there were those back home who frequently remembered him in their prayers. This gave him courage to go on and to hope more strongly in the God who had called him to go to India in the first place. Carey wrote in his diary: "I feel that it is good to commit my soul, my body, and my all into the hands of God. Then the world appears little, the promise is great, and God an all-sufficient portion."

Bearing the Mark of Jesus

In "Anxious Times"

A new command I give you: Love one another.
As I have loved you, so you must love one another. All men
will know that you are my disciples if you love one another.

JOHN 13:34–35

May they be brought to complete unity to let the world know that
you sent me and have loved them even as you have loved me.

JOHN 17:23

The world has not seen the beginning of what Jesus indicates is the
final apologetic—observable oneness among true Christians
who are truly brothers and sisters in Christ.

FRANCIS SCHAEFFER

John Lennon's "Imagine" continues to fascinate and inspire. Lennon envisioned a world of peace—but also a world without religion. Lennon apparently believed religion inevitably stirred up conflict and war. Consequently, he could find no room in his world for Jesus Christ, who Christians believe is the true source of peace, the "Prince of Peace."

The lyrics of Lennon's *Imagine* may fascinate, but they also disturb. Even "secular" persons acknowledge that the dream of a world without religion is probably an illusion. "Religion" does not appear to be withering away any time soon, especially outside of Europe, North America, and Australia. Conservative expressions of the Christian faith are expanding rapidly in Latin America, Africa, and Asia.

For that matter, Islam is also making considerable advances—in Africa, Europe, and other parts of the world. A recent *Chicago Tribune* report noted the growing influence of Islam within Egypt. For a number of decades "a conservative Islamic revival has been quietly transforming the nation's culture and society." Many formerly "moderate" or "westernized" Egyptian women are once again wearing the *hijah,* a veil signifying their desire to follow a more strict form of Islam. Egyptian men are proud of *zabitas,* callused bumps on their foreheads caused by hitting their heads on the ground during prayers.[1] Indeed, the advance of Islam as well as that of other faiths deflates the "secularization" hypothesis so widely touted in the 1960s and 1970s.

Commentators like Philip Jenkins, while appreciating the benefits of "religion," are concerned about the potential for mayhem that can result from clashes between religions and sects. He observes: "The twenty-first century will be regarded by future historians as a century in which religion replaced ideology as the prime animating and destructive force in human affairs." John Lennon's indictment that religion can be a source of conflict was not itself an illusion.

Since the surprise attacks of September 11, 2001, and in part due to destructive conflicts between various representatives of world religions and sects, a number of observers believe we have entered into an "anxious times." In the United States, scholars, clerics, and others are engaged in discussions regarding how we should live in this new age of anxiety. A few commentators have wondered aloud, "What will save us?"

THE GOD "OUT THERE"

At a "Forum on Religion in the 2004 Election" held in Washington, D.C. (March 2004 and sponsored by "The Interfaith Alliance"), notable mainstream scholars discussed the role of religion in American political life. One of the participants, James A. Forbes, poignantly described the anxiety factor that he believed hovered over political life in this country.

He contended that Americans are very worried about their personal safety and their futures: "We are all asking what is our responsibility in determining the conditions that make us safe. We are all asking who can save us. . . . Is there anybody out there that can save us religiously? So we're all asking those questions. And how do we contain our anxiety and deal with our fears in a way that makes it possible to get up, go to work, take care of our families?"

Forbes wondered if "God" can give us meaning and hope in these "anxious times": "Something has got to happen to help us decide is there anybody out there, does that out there person have some sense of the values that are right and wrong, and can we, if we embrace those values, look forward to more meaningful life, a better sense of personal and national purpose, and can we enjoy our families and give our kids some hope for the future? So I think maybe God's got to be our big teacher, because we're all in school on religious matters these days."[2]

As evangelical Christians, we have good news to give to all those in this "school on religious matters." The God "out there" has already revealed the answer to life's problems, including not only our anxieties, but also our need for salvation from sin. This answer is found in the person and work of Jesus Christ and in Holy Scripture.

If this is so, why do non-Christians often seem so hesitant to consider Christ's gospel? In this book we have proposed that one major reason is that they do not always see in us the mark of Jesus. Put another way, they are not convinced that we are authentic disciples of Jesus Christ. For them, this perception often disqualifies us from being suitable ambassadors for Christ and His gospel.

SHOWING RESPECT AND LOVE

The red lights of the cameras went off. Thrilled by how well the debate had apparently unfolded, the evangelical spokesperson stepped off the television set. He approached his son who had watched the hard-hitting exchanges from behind the cameras. "Well, son, how do you think I did?" The twenty-something young man replied: "You were great, Dad. You destroyed the woman's arguments. It was a clear-cut win."

Knowing that his son was probably holding back another assessment, the father continued: "OK, how do you think I *really* did?" With a pained expression, the son looked up at his dad. He then answered: "Dad, you won all right, but by your attitude you lost any future chance ever to speak again to the woman about Christ."

The father became crestfallen. He knew that his own son was struggling with the Christian faith, having seen too much hypocrisy and pride displayed by so-called "television personalities." Now he, the father, was adding his own example of how Christians sometimes treat others without respect, dignity, and love.

A few years later the father recounted this story to one of the present authors. He indicated that it was in the context of the conversation with his son that he arrived at a very unsettling insight. His failure to show respect and genuine love for others of different convictions constituted not only a stumbling block for them, but also for his own son. The father determined that, henceforth in his ministry and wholly dependent upon the power of the Holy Spirit, he must bear the "mark of Jesus"—even in debates with persons who appeared unfriendly, if not dismissive of the faith and of himself.

Interestingly enough, Francis Schaeffer (1912–1984) had gone through a similar crisis experience in his own ministry. An admirer of J. Gresham Machen, Schaeffer began studies at Westminster Theological Seminary in 1935. He saw firsthand the struggles of the fundamentalist-modernist controversy. He was greatly concerned when Machen was put on trial and defrocked for refusing to disband the Independent Mission Board (see chapter 5). In fact, after World War II, Schaeffer represented the Independent Mission Board in Europe.

In 1951, Schaeffer, a Presbyterian separatist, determined to devote more time to the defense of the faith. He indicated that he "felt a strong burden to stand for the historical Christian position, and for the purity of the faith." At the same time, Schaeffer was overtaken by a spiritual crisis. It was precipitated in part by his personal experience in what he thought were unseemly denominational battles involving his own orthodox, separatist colleagues. He realized that he had acquired a critical spirit. He confessed that he lacked a sense of the reality and joy of the Christian faith.

SCHAEFFER'S MARK OF LOVE

Troubled in soul, Francis Schaeffer devoted himself to reading Scripture and prayer. He came to a new understanding of the importance of the work of the Holy Spirit in sanctification. He grasped that his efforts to defend the Christian faith, however well conceived, would be compromised if he did not demonstrate love to other Christians and to non-Christians. With the Lord's strength he began to love people whom he had previously thought were impossible to love.

In 1955, Francis Schaeffer established *L'Abri* at Chalet les Mélèzes in Huémoz, Switzerland. It became a center where prayer, Bible study, fellowship, and unconditional love were present in large supplies. At *L'Abri*, meaning "shelter" in French, many a young person did find shelter from the ravages and loneliness of an uncaring world. Whatever their tattered and sinful background may have been, Edith and Francis Schaeffer and their staff greeted them with the love of Christ and took them into the "shelter."

The Schaeffers spent time listening to their guests—many of whom had painful experiences to recount. Francis Schaeffer provided them with the gospel message and insightful cultural critiques of other worldviews. He patiently answered their objections to the Christian faith, if they had any. He was well prepared to do so. During his recent spiritual crisis, Schaeffer had rethought his own "reasons for being a Christian." "I saw again that there were totally sufficient reasons to know that the infinite-personal God does exist and that Christianity is true." At *L'Abri*, scores of young people found the true peace for which they had been looking in Jesus Christ, the Prince of Peace.

Anky Rookmaaker, whose husband Hans Rookmaaker (d. 1977) was a renowned art historian at the University of Amsterdam, testified to the spiritual impact of *L'Abri* upon herself and others: "Many people think of L'Abri as a Christian work for intellectuals; and it is true that many intellectuals found answers to their questions and Christ as the

Savior at L'Abri. But I am not an intellectual, and I never felt out of place at L'Abri. . . . I have always felt accepted and loved, not only by Francis and Edith Schaeffer, but also by the younger generation of L'Abri workers and members. I love my church in Holland, but I feel at home at L'Abri."[3]

When Francis Schaeffer wrote *The Mark of the Christian,* he felt a certain freedom to call upon Christians to embrace the "untried" apologetic of bearing the "mark of a Christian." Why did he have such freedom? His admonition had no touch of hypocrisy about it. With the power of the Holy Spirit, Schaeffer had been attempting to evidence *seeable, costly* love to others himself.

THE SEARCH FOR SHELTER

In these "anxious times," with news ranging from terrorism to tsunamis, many people are looking for "shelter." They are searching for people who will display a seeable, costly love and care for them without ulterior motives. It is absolutely stunning how many people, even if they enjoy outward "success" and access to large sums of money, are lonely. Even in a crowd, they can live lives of quiet desperation.

As evangelicals, we should bear the "mark of Jesus" and be shelter givers. Through the power of the Holy Spirit, we should seek to fulfill Christ's command to love our neighbors as ourselves, whether they are Christians or not (John 13:34–35).

May we be moved by compassion to present the gospel of Jesus Christ to others in a loving and respectful manner. And may our love for each other afford a visible demonstration of the unity of the body of Christ, such that the watching world might believe that the Father sent the Son (John 17:23). It is He who is our matchless Redeemer and Savior, Jesus Christ. He is the Good Shepherd, who shelters His lambs in His loving arms (John 10:14; Isaiah 40:11).

Notes

Introduction
Imagine: A World Without God

1. Philip Jenkins, "The Next Christianity," *The Atlantic Online* (October 2002): 6, http://www.theatlantic.com/doc/200210/jenkins. See also Philip Jenkins, *The Next Christendom: The Coming of Global Christianity* (New York: Oxford, 2002).

2. Leo D. Lefebure, *Revelation, the Religions, and Violence* (New York: Orbis, 2000), 7.

3. "Révélations du philosophe catholique Jean Guitton," *Paris Match* (no date given); interview with Igor Bogdanoff and Grichka Bogdanoff.

4. Charles Simic, "Down There on a Visit," *The New York Review of Books* 51 (12 August 2004): 46.

5. Ibid., 47.

6. Ross Douthat, "The God Vote," *The Atlantic,* September 2004, 52.

7. Francis Schaeffer, *The Mark of the Christian* (L'Abri Fellowship, 1970), 29; http://www.ccel.us/schaeffer.html.

Chapter 1
The Christian's Mark

1. As quoted in J. I. Packer and Thomas C. Oden, *One Faith: The Evangelical Consensus* (Downers Grove, Ill.: InterVarsity, 2004), 194.

2. D. Martyn Lloyd-Jones; *Studies in the Sermon on the Mount* (Grand Rapids: Eerdmans, 1984), 214–15.

3. St. Augustine, *The Confessions,* Henry Chadwick, trans. (Oxford, England: Oxford Univ. Press, 1991), 2.2.2 and 2.7.15.

Chapter 2
Loving Your Neighbor When It Seems Impossible

1. Francis Schaeffer, *The Mark of the Christian* (L'Abri Fellowship, 1970), 29, http://www.ccel.us/schaeffer.html.

2. Ibid., 15, 22.

3. Lewis Smedes, "A Legacy of Wisdom: Memorable Lewis Smedes Quotations," *Fuller Focus,* summer 2003, 7.

4. Jonathan Edwards, *Thoughts on the Revival in New England,* Part IV (New York: n.p., 1832), 274–75.

5. Correspondence from Kenneth Klassen to John Woodbridge, 20 March 2004.

6. Minna M. Rowney, *Star Phoenix,* Editorial Section, Letter Box 24, November 1971; cited in Ken Klassen, "The Long-Term Effects of the Canadian Revival of 1971 on Ebenezer Baptist, Saskatoon, SK" (paper for DMN923A, Revivals and Revivalism, Trinity Evangelical Divinity School, 6 June 2003), 21.

7. Correspondence from Peter Cha to John Woodbridge, 15 March 2004.

8. Clarence Page, "Unspoken Conflicts," *Chicago Tribune,* 8 February 2004, opinion page.

9. Thomas C. Holt, *The Problem of Race in the Twenty-First Century* (Cambridge, Mass.: Harvard Univ. Press), 110.

10. Andrew F. Walls, *The Cross-Cultural Process in Christian History* (Maryknoll, N.Y.: Orbis, 2002), 69.

11. R. Stephen Warner, "Coming to America: Immigrants and the Faith They Bring," *Christian Century,* 10 February 2004, 23.

12. Jeanette Yep et al., *Following Jesus Without Dishonoring Your Parents* (Downers Grove, Ill.: InterVarsity, 1998).

13. Orlando Crespo, *Being Latino in Christ* (Downers Grove, Ill.: InterVarsity, 2003).

14. Glenn C. Loury, *The Anatomy of Racial Inequality* (Cambridge, Mass.: Harvard Univ. Press, 2003), 175–204.

15. Glenn C. Loury, *One by One from the Inside Out: Essays and Reviews on Race and Responsibility in America* (New York: Free Press, 1995), 320.

Chapter 3
Evangelical Unity
Drawing Boundaries and Crossing Barriers

1. Konrad Reiser, "Thirty Years in the Service of the Ecumenical Movement: The Joint Working Group Between the Roman Catholic Church and the World Council of Churches," an address to that Joint Working Group, Rome, 4 April 1995; as quoted by Cardinal Edward Cassidy, "The Churches and Ecumenism Today," public lecture given at Seton Hall University, July 1996.

2. John H. Leith, *The Reformed Imperative* (Louisville, Kent.: Westminister John Knox, 1988), 22.

3. Tertullian, "Apology," xxxix, S. Thelwall, trans., in *Ante-Nicene Fathers,* Alexander Roberts and James Donaldson, eds. (1885; repr. Peabody, Mass.: Hendrickson, 2004), 46.

4. Francis Schaeffer, *The Mark of the Christian* (Downers Grove, Ill.: InterVarsity, 1977), 22.

Chapter 4
When the World Calls Us Hypocrites
How Should We Respond?

1. Molly Ivins, "Kissinger Back at His Game: Covering Up," *Chicago Tribune,* 12 December 2002, opinion page.

2. Kathleen Parker, "Dissecting the Makings of a Christian Jihadist," *Chicago Tribune,* 17 November 2004, opinion page.

3. Nicholas D. Kristof, "God, Satan and The Media,"*New York Times,* 4 March 2003, A27.

4. Don Wycliff, "Challenging the Media's 'Pro-Gay' Tenor," *Chicago Tribune,* 8 July 2004, opinion page.

5. George Marsden, *The Soul of the American University from Protestant Establishment to Established Nonbelief* (New York: Oxford Univ. Press, 1994), 430.

6. Charles Spurgeon, *Morning and Evening Daily Readings* (Grand Rapids: Hendrikson, 1998), 9.

7. "The First Apology of Justin the Martyr," *Early Christian Fathers,* Cyril C. Richardson, ed. (New York: MacMillan, 1970), 249–50.

8. As quoted in Tim Stafford, "The Third Coming of George Barna," *Christianity Today,* 5 August, 2002, 38.

9. Christian Smith, *American Evangelicalism: Embattled and Thriving* (Chicago: Univ. of Chicago Press, 1998), 39.

10. Spurgeon, *Morning and Evening,* 16.

11. Hugh Heclo, "The Wall That Never Was," *The Wilson Quarterly* (Winter 2003): 68–82.

12. Spurgeon, *Morning and Evening,* 64.

Chapter 5
What's in a Name
Are We All Fundamentalists?

1. Vincent J. Schodolski, "Islamic Scholar Takes on Fundamentalists," *Chicago Tribune,* 25 November 2002, opinion page.

2. Henry Emerson Fosdick, "Shall the Fundamentalists Win?" *Christian Work,* 102 (June 10, 1922): 716–722.

3. On Fosdick's career, see: Robert Moatsmiller, *Harry Emerson Fosdick: Preacher, Pastor, Prophet* (New York: Oxford Univ. Press, 1925).

4. Curtis Lee Laws, "Convention Side Lights," *Watchman-Examiner,* 8 (1 July 1920): 834.

5. James M. Gray, "The Deadline of Doctrine around the Church," *Moody Monthly,* November 1922, 101.

6. J. Gresham Machen, *Christianity and Liberalism* (New York: MacMillan, 1923), 48–49.

7. Reinhold Niebuhr, "Our Secularized Civilization," *Christian Century,* 22 April 1927.

8. Harold Ockenga, "The Unvoiced Multitudes," *Evangelical Action: A Report of the Organization of the National Association of Evangelicals for United Action* (Boston: United Action, 1942), 32–33.

9. Carl F. H. Henry, *Evangelicals in Search of Identity* (Waco, Tex.: Word, 1976), 41, 48.

10. John Fea, "Come Out from Among Them: Separatist Fundamentalism in America 1941–1991" (masters thesis in Church History, Trinity Evangelical Divinity School, 1992), 4.

11. George Marsden, *Fundamentalism and American Culture: The Shaping of the Twentieth Century, 1870–1925* (Waco, Tex.: Word, 1980), 227.

12. Martin E. Marty, "Fundamentalism Reborn: Faith and Fanaticism," *Saturday Review* (May 1980), 37.

13. Peter Berger, ed., *The Desecularization of World Resurgent Religion and World Politics* (Grand Rapids: Eerdman's, 1999) 1–2.

14. Peter G. Bientenholz, annotator, *The Correspondence of Erasmus* (Toronto: Univ. of Toronto Press, 1979), 5:289–90.

15. Augustine, *The Letters of St. Augustine*, 28:3:3, in *New Advent: Fathers of the Church*, www.newadvent.org/fathers/1102028.htm.

16. Ibid., 82:1:3, www.newadvent.org/fathers/1102082.htm.

17. John H. Dietrich, "Who Are These Fundamentalists?" *The Humanist Pulpit* (1926).

18. Arthur Bennett, ed., *The Valley of Vision: A Collection of Puritan Prayers and Devotions* (Carlisle, Pa.: Banner of Truth, 2002), 169.

Chapter 6
But What About
People of Other Religions?

1. Lesslie Newbigin, *The Gospel in the Pluralist Society* (Grand Rapids: Eerdmans, 1989), 159.

2. "Southern Baptist Missionaries: Back Off Islam," Religious News Service, quoted in *The Alabama Baptist*, 6 February 2003.

3. William Ernest Hocking, *Living Religions and a World Faith* (New York: MacMillan, 1940), 231.

4. Robert Sullivan, *Holy Lands: One Place, Three Faiths*, introduction by Thomas Cahill (New York: Life Books, 2002).

5. Simone Weil, *Waiting for God* (1951; repr., San Francisco: Harper and Row, 1973), 69.

6. Timothy George, *Faithful Witness: The Life and Mission of William Carey* (Dothan, Ala.: New Hope, 1991), 166–67.

7. Carey was speaking in Calcutta to the Baptist Missionary Society on 25 November 1793; quoted in Eustace Carey, *Memoir of William Carey* (1836; repr., Hartford: Robins and Smith, 1844), iii.

8. As quoted in George Smith, *The Life of William Carey, Shoemaker and Missionary* (London: John Murray, 1887), 118.

9. As quoted in J. I. Packer and Thomas C. Oden, *One Faith: The Evangelical Consensus* (Downers Grove, Ill.: InterVarsity, 2004), 196.

Conclusion
Bearing the Mark of Jesus
In "Anxious Times"

1. Lisa Anderson, "Egypt's Cultural Shift Reflects Islam's Pull," *Chicago Tribune,* 21 March 2004.

2. "'Faith Vote' Realities," A Forum on Religion in the 2004 Election (17 March 2004), 2; at http://www.interfaithalliance.org/site/pp.asp?c=8dJll-WMCE&b=120842.

3. Lane T. Dennis, ed. *Francis A. Schaeffer: Portraits of the Man and His Work* (Westchester, Ill.: Crossway, 1986), 161.

SINCE 1894, Moody Publishers has been dedicated to equip and motivate people to advance the cause of Christ by publishing evangelical Christian literature and other media for all ages, around the world. Because we are a ministry of the Moody Bible Institute of Chicago, a portion of the proceeds from the sale of this book go to train the next generation of Christian leaders.

If we may serve you in any way in your spiritual journey toward understanding Christ and the Christian life, please contact us at www.moodypublishers.com.

"All Scripture is God-breathed and is useful for teaching, rebuking, correcting and training in righteousness, so that the man of God may be thoroughly equipped for every good work."
—2 TIMOTHY 3:16, 17

MOODY
PUBLISHERS

THE NAME YOU CAN TRUST®

THE MARK OF JESUS TEAM

ACQUIRING EDITOR
Mark Tobey

COPY EDITOR
Jim Vincent

BACK COVER COPY
Lisa Ann Cockrel

COVER DESIGN
UDG DesignWorks
www.thedesignworksgroup.com

COVER PHOTO
Image Club Graphics

INTERIOR DESIGN
BlueFrog Design

PRINTING AND BINDING
Versa Press, Inc.

The typeface for the text of this book is
AGaramond